D0584693

THIS JOURNAL BELONGS TO:

_____

PURPOSE

EVERYONE HAS THEIR OWN UNIQUE SET OF TALENTS, INTERESTS, AND LIFE EXPERIENCES THAT BRING THEM JOY OR GIVE THEM A REASON TO GET UP IN THE MORNING. LEARNING TO RECOGNIZE WHAT TALENTS YOU HAVE AND WHAT YOU LOVE TO DO CAN SET YOU ON THE PATH OF FINDING YOUR PURPOSE AND LIVING YOUR BEST LIFE.

FINDING ONE'S PERSONAL PURPOSE IS ESSENTIAL FOR HAPPY, HEALTHY LIVING. It can provide you with stability and direction to sustain you through life's challenges and setbacks, and it can make you feel more connected to others, by using your gifts to do good in the world.

We often have preconceived ideas about our purpose in life—get married, have kids, earn a certain amount of money, or achieve a certain position in society. These types of achievements, however, often do not bring the kind of fulfillment that comes with finding your personal sense of purpose. Ideally, your purpose blends with your interests, brings you joy, and has an ongoing impact on the world, whether large or small.

Sometimes it can be hard to recognize the things we are good at or most passionate about because they have become ingrained in our everyday life and thinking. The following pages contain questions and exercises designed to help you start thinking about what skills and talents you have, what excites and inspires you most, what you are passionate about, and what your life's purpose might be.

DISCOVERING YOUR PURPOSE

DISCOVERING YOUR PURPOSE

WHAT I LOVED TO DO AS A CHILD:

_____

_____

_____

_____

I'M HAPPIEST / FEEL MOST ALIVE WHEN I'M DOING THIS:

_____

_____

_____

_____

_____

I CAN DO THIS FOR HOURS ON END:

_____

_____

_____

_____

I'M PASSIONATE ABOUT:

_____

_____

_____

_____

_____

I'M REALLY GOOD AT:

_____   _____
_____   _____
_____   _____
_____   _____

THINGS THAT OTHERS THINK I'M REALLY GOOD AT:

_____   _____
_____   _____
_____   _____
_____   _____

THE UNIQUE QUALITIES THAT I HAVE:

_____   _____
_____   _____
_____   _____

WHAT I LOVE MOST ABOUT MYSELF:

_____
_____
_____
_____

WHAT MAKES ME FEEL PROUD:

_____
_____
_____
_____

DISCOVERING YOUR PURPOSE

MY CORE VALUES:

_____

_____

_____

_____

_____

_____

_____

_____

_____

_____

_____

_____

_____

REAL WORLD ISSUES THAT CONCERN ME:

_____

_____

_____

_____

_____

_____

_____

_____

HOW I CAN USE MY TALENTS TO SERVE HUMANITY:

_____

_____

_____

_____

_____

_____

A UNIQUE CHALLENGE I'VE HAD TO OVERCOME, AND
HOW I CAN HELP OTHERS FROM WHAT I'VE LEARNED:

_____

_____

_____

_____

_____

I'VE WASTED TIME/
ENERGY ON:

_____

_____

_____

_____

I'D LIKE TO SPEND
MORE TIME ON:

_____

_____

_____

_____

PEOPLE THAT INSPIRE ME:

_____ _____ _____

_____ _____ _____

_____ _____ _____

DISCOVERING YOUR PURPOSE

MY LIFE FEELS IDEAL WHEN I AM:
(Mark your top 5 responses when your list is complete.)

01 _____

02 _____

03 _____

04 _____

05 _____

06 _____

07 _____

08 _____

09 _____

10 _____

LIFE'S PURPOSE VISION STATEMENT

STEP 1: Use the following page to summarize what you have discovered so far about your purpose and to record your responses to the 5 purpose prompts below. These key takeaways serve to form the draft for your personal vision statement.

1. Your strengths and passion.
2. Your core principles and values.
3. Skills you have that can solve real-world issues.
4. The role you want to have and why.
5. Short and long-term goals you'd like to accomplish.

WHAT I'VE DISCOVERED ABOUT MY LIFE'S PURPOSE:

_____
_____
_____
_____
_____
_____
_____
_____
_____
_____
_____
_____
_____
_____
_____
_____
_____

MY LIFE'S PURPOSE VISION STATEMENT:

_____
_____
_____
_____
_____
_____
_____
_____
_____

90-DAY
PURPOSE
JOURNAL

Now that you have gained more clarity about your interests, skills, and passions, use the pages of this journal to start being mindful of living your life's purpose. Take your time. You don't have to completely overhaul your life all at once. Start living your purpose a bit more fully every day, and pay attention to the results you are producing, how you are feeling, and the contribution you are making to the world.

MORNING REFLECTION

DATE ___ / ___ /___

MY PURPOSE OR INTENTION FOR TODAY:

_____

_____

_____

GOALS ALIGNED WITH MY PURPOSE:

_____   _____

_____   _____

_____   _____

ACTION STEPS I CAN TAKE TODAY:

☐ _____   ☐ _____

☐ _____   ☐ _____

☐ _____   ☐ _____

A SELF-CARE GOAL FOR TODAY:

_____

_____

A CHALLENGE I'M FACING: SOMETHING I'M EXCITED ABOUT:

_____   _____

_____   _____

HOW I SPENT MY TIME TODAY:

☐ MY LIFE'S PASSION   ☐ WORKING   ☐ TIME WITH FRIENDS/FAMILY

☐ VOLUNTEERING   ☐ SELF-CARE   ☐ TIME OUTDOORS

☐ ONLINE/SOCIAL MEDIA   ☐ DOWN TIME   ☐ OTHER: _____

EVENING REFLECTION

HOW I'M FEELING:

_____

_____

_____

THIS BROUGHT ME THE GREATEST JOY TODAY:

_____

_____

SOMETHING I DID TODAY THAT FELT MEANINGFUL:

_____

_____

_____

WHAT I DID TODAY THAT ALIGNED WITH MY PURPOSE:

_____

_____

_____

A NOTABLE RESULT FROM LIVING MY PURPOSE:

_____

_____

_____

A SETBACK I FACED TODAY AND HOW
I CAN LEARN OR GROW FROM THIS:

_____

_____

_____

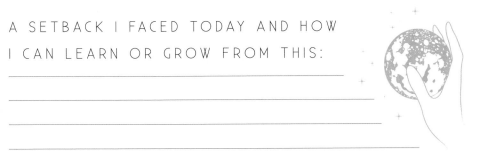

MORNING REFLECTION

DATE ___/___/___

MY PURPOSE OR INTENTION FOR TODAY:

_____

_____

_____

GOALS ALIGNED WITH MY PURPOSE:

_____   _____

_____   _____

_____   _____

ACTION STEPS I CAN TAKE TODAY:

☐ _____   ☐ _____

☐ _____   ☐ _____

☐ _____   ☐ _____

A SELF-CARE GOAL FOR TODAY:

_____

_____

A CHALLENGE I'M FACING: SOMETHING I'M EXCITED ABOUT:

_____   _____

_____   _____

_____   _____

HOW I SPENT MY TIME TODAY:

☐ MY LIFE'S PASSION   ☐ WORKING   ☐ TIME WITH FRIENDS/FAMILY

☐ VOLUNTEERING   ☐ SELF-CARE   ☐ TIME OUTDOORS

☐ ONLINE/SOCIAL MEDIA   ☐ DOWN TIME   ☐ OTHER: _____

EVENING REFLECTION

HOW I'M FEELING:

_____
_____
_____

THIS BROUGHT ME THE GREATEST JOY TODAY:

_____
_____

SOMETHING I DID TODAY THAT FELT MEANINGFUL:

_____
_____
_____

WHAT I DID TODAY THAT ALIGNED WITH MY PURPOSE:

_____
_____
_____

A NOTABLE RESULT FROM LIVING MY PURPOSE:

_____
_____
_____

A SETBACK I FACED TODAY AND HOW
I CAN LEARN OR GROW FROM THIS:

_____
_____
_____
_____

MORNING REFLECTION

DATE ___ / ___ /

MY PURPOSE OR INTENTION FOR TODAY:

_____

_____

_____

GOALS ALIGNED WITH MY PURPOSE:

_____   _____

_____   _____

_____   _____

ACTION STEPS I CAN TAKE TODAY:

☐ _____   ☐ _____

☐ _____   ☐ _____

☐ _____   ☐ _____

A SELF-CARE GOAL FOR TODAY:

_____

_____

A CHALLENGE I'M FACING:

_____

_____

_____

SOMETHING I'M EXCITED ABOUT:

_____

_____

_____

HOW I SPENT MY TIME TODAY:

☐ MY LIFE'S PASSION   ☐ WORKING   ☐ TIME WITH FRIENDS/FAMILY

☐ VOLUNTEERING   ☐ SELF-CARE   ☐ TIME OUTDOORS

☐ ONLINE/SOCIAL MEDIA   ☐ DOWN TIME   ☐ OTHER: _____

EVENING REFLECTION

HOW I'M FEELING:

_____

_____

_____

THIS BROUGHT ME THE GREATEST JOY TODAY:

_____

_____

SOMETHING I DID TODAY THAT FELT MEANINGFUL:

_____

_____

_____

WHAT I DID TODAY THAT ALIGNED WITH MY PURPOSE:

_____

_____

_____

A NOTABLE RESULT FROM LIVING MY PURPOSE:

_____

_____

_____

A SETBACK I FACED TODAY AND HOW
I CAN LEARN OR GROW FROM THIS:

_____

_____

_____

_____

MORNING REFLECTION

DATE ___/___/___

MY PURPOSE OR INTENTION FOR TODAY:

_____

_____

_____

GOALS ALIGNED WITH MY PURPOSE:

_____   _____

_____   _____

_____   _____

ACTION STEPS I CAN TAKE TODAY:

☐ _____   ☐ _____

☐ _____   ☐ _____

☐ _____   ☐ _____

A SELF-CARE GOAL FOR TODAY:

_____

_____

A CHALLENGE I'M FACING: SOMETHING I'M EXCITED ABOUT:

_____   _____

_____   _____

_____   _____

HOW I SPENT MY TIME TODAY:

☐ MY LIFE'S PASSION   ☐ WORKING   ☐ TIME WITH FRIENDS/FAMILY

☐ VOLUNTEERING   ☐ SELF-CARE   ☐ TIME OUTDOORS

☐ ONLINE/SOCIAL MEDIA   ☐ DOWN TIME   ☐ OTHER: _____

EVENING REFLECTION

HOW I'M FEELING:

_____

_____

_____

THIS BROUGHT ME THE GREATEST JOY TODAY:

_____

_____

SOMETHING I DID TODAY THAT FELT MEANINGFUL:

_____

_____

WHAT I DID TODAY THAT ALIGNED WITH MY PURPOSE:

_____

_____

_____

A NOTABLE RESULT FROM LIVING MY PURPOSE:

_____

_____

_____

A SETBACK I FACED TODAY AND HOW
I CAN LEARN OR GROW FROM THIS:

_____

_____

_____

MORNING REFLECTION

DATE ___ / ___ / ___

MY PURPOSE OR INTENTION FOR TODAY:

_____

_____

_____

GOALS ALIGNED WITH MY PURPOSE:

_____   _____

_____   _____

_____   _____

ACTION STEPS I CAN TAKE TODAY:

☐ _____   ☐ _____

☐ _____   ☐ _____

☐ _____   ☐ _____

A SELF-CARE GOAL FOR TODAY:

_____

_____

A CHALLENGE I'M FACING: SOMETHING I'M EXCITED ABOUT:

_____   _____

_____   _____

HOW I SPENT MY TIME TODAY:

☐ MY LIFE'S PASSION   ☐ WORKING   ☐ TIME WITH FRIENDS/FAMILY

☐ VOLUNTEERING   ☐ SELF-CARE   ☐ TIME OUTDOORS

☐ ONLINE/SOCIAL MEDIA   ☐ DOWN TIME   ☐ OTHER: _____

EVENING REFLECTION

HOW I'M FEELING:

_____

_____

_____

THIS BROUGHT ME THE GREATEST JOY TODAY:

_____

_____

SOMETHING I DID TODAY THAT FELT MEANINGFUL:

_____

_____

_____

WHAT I DID TODAY THAT ALIGNED WITH MY PURPOSE:

_____

_____

_____

A NOTABLE RESULT FROM LIVING MY PURPOSE:

_____

_____

_____

A SETBACK I FACED TODAY AND HOW
I CAN LEARN OR GROW FROM THIS:

_____

_____

_____

MORNING REFLECTION

DATE ___/___/___

MY PURPOSE OR INTENTION FOR TODAY:

_____

_____

_____

GOALS ALIGNED WITH MY PURPOSE:

_____   _____

_____   _____

ACTION STEPS I CAN TAKE TODAY:

☐ _____   ☐ _____

☐ _____   ☐ _____

☐ _____   ☐ _____

A SELF-CARE GOAL FOR TODAY:

_____

_____

A CHALLENGE I'M FACING:

_____

_____

_____

SOMETHING I'M EXCITED ABOUT:

_____

_____

_____

HOW I SPENT MY TIME TODAY:

☐ MY LIFE'S PASSION   ☐ WORKING   ☐ TIME WITH FRIENDS/FAMILY

☐ VOLUNTEERING   ☐ SELF-CARE   ☐ TIME OUTDOORS

☐ ONLINE/SOCIAL MEDIA   ☐ DOWN TIME   ☐ OTHER: _____

EVENING REFLECTION

HOW I'M FEELING:

_____

_____

_____

THIS BROUGHT ME THE GREATEST JOY TODAY:

_____

_____

SOMETHING I DID TODAY THAT FELT MEANINGFUL:

_____

_____

_____

WHAT I DID TODAY THAT ALIGNED WITH MY PURPOSE:

_____

_____

_____

A NOTABLE RESULT FROM LIVING MY PURPOSE:

_____

_____

_____

A SETBACK I FACED TODAY AND HOW
I CAN LEARN OR GROW FROM THIS:

_____

_____

_____

_____

MORNING REFLECTION

DATE ___/___/___

MY PURPOSE OR INTENTION FOR TODAY:

_____
_____
_____

GOALS ALIGNED WITH MY PURPOSE:

_____   _____
_____   _____
_____   _____

ACTION STEPS I CAN TAKE TODAY:

☐ _____   ☐ _____
☐ _____   ☐ _____
☐ _____   ☐ _____

A SELF-CARE GOAL FOR TODAY:

_____
_____
_____

A CHALLENGE I'M FACING:

_____

_____

_____

SOMETHING I'M EXCITED ABOUT:

_____

_____

_____

HOW I SPENT MY TIME TODAY:

☐ MY LIFE'S PASSION   ☐ WORKING   ☐ TIME WITH FRIENDS/FAMILY
☐ VOLUNTEERING   ☐ SELF-CARE   ☐ TIME OUTDOORS
☐ ONLINE/SOCIAL MEDIA   ☐ DOWN TIME   ☐ OTHER:_____

EVENING REFLECTION

HOW I'M FEELING:

_____

_____

_____

THIS BROUGHT ME THE GREATEST JOY TODAY:

_____

_____

SOMETHING I DID TODAY THAT FELT MEANINGFUL:

_____

_____

_____

WHAT I DID TODAY THAT ALIGNED WITH MY PURPOSE:

_____

_____

_____

A NOTABLE RESULT FROM LIVING MY PURPOSE:

_____

_____

_____

A SETBACK I FACED TODAY AND HOW
I CAN LEARN OR GROW FROM THIS:

_____

_____

_____

_____

MORNING REFLECTION

DATE ___ / ___ / ___

MY PURPOSE OR INTENTION FOR TODAY:

_____
_____
_____

GOALS ALIGNED WITH MY PURPOSE:

_____   _____
_____   _____

ACTION STEPS I CAN TAKE TODAY:

☐ _____   ☐ _____
☐ _____   ☐ _____
☐ _____   ☐ _____

A SELF-CARE GOAL FOR TODAY:

_____
_____

A CHALLENGE I'M FACING: SOMETHING I'M EXCITED ABOUT:

_____   _____
_____   _____
_____   _____

HOW I SPENT MY TIME TODAY:

☐ MY LIFE'S PASSION   ☐ WORKING   ☐ TIME WITH FRIENDS/FAMILY
☐ VOLUNTEERING   ☐ SELF-CARE   ☐ TIME OUTDOORS
☐ ONLINE/SOCIAL MEDIA   ☐ DOWN TIME   ☐ OTHER: _____

EVENING REFLECTION

HOW I'M FEELING:

_____

_____

_____

THIS BROUGHT ME THE GREATEST JOY TODAY:

_____

_____

SOMETHING I DID TODAY THAT FELT MEANINGFUL:

_____

_____

_____

WHAT I DID TODAY THAT ALIGNED WITH MY PURPOSE:

_____

_____

_____

A NOTABLE RESULT FROM LIVING MY PURPOSE:

_____

_____

_____

A SETBACK I FACED TODAY AND HOW
I CAN LEARN OR GROW FROM THIS:

_____

_____

_____

MORNING REFLECTION

DATE ___ / ___ / ___

MY PURPOSE OR INTENTION FOR TODAY:
_____
_____
_____

GOALS ALIGNED WITH MY PURPOSE:
_____ _____
_____ _____
_____ _____

ACTION STEPS I CAN TAKE TODAY:
☐ _____ ☐ _____
☐ _____ ☐ _____
☐ _____ ☐ _____

A SELF-CARE GOAL FOR TODAY:
_____
_____

A CHALLENGE I'M FACING: SOMETHING I'M EXCITED ABOUT:
_____ _____
_____ _____
_____ _____

HOW I SPENT MY TIME TODAY:

☐ MY LIFE'S PASSION   ☐ WORKING   ☐ TIME WITH FRIENDS/FAMILY
☐ VOLUNTEERING   ☐ SELF-CARE   ☐ TIME OUTDOORS
☐ ONLINE/SOCIAL MEDIA   ☐ DOWN TIME   ☐ OTHER: _____

EVENING REFLECTION

HOW I'M FEELING:

_____

_____

_____

THIS BROUGHT ME THE GREATEST JOY TODAY:

_____

_____

SOMETHING I DID TODAY THAT FELT MEANINGFUL:

_____

_____

_____

WHAT I DID TODAY THAT ALIGNED WITH MY PURPOSE:

_____

_____

_____

A NOTABLE RESULT FROM LIVING MY PURPOSE:

_____

_____

_____

A SETBACK I FACED TODAY AND HOW
I CAN LEARN OR GROW FROM THIS:

_____

_____

_____

_____

MORNING REFLECTION

DATE ____/____/____

MY PURPOSE OR INTENTION FOR TODAY:

_____

_____

_____

GOALS ALIGNED WITH MY PURPOSE:

_____   _____

_____   _____

_____   _____

ACTION STEPS I CAN TAKE TODAY:

☐ _____   ☐ _____

☐ _____   ☐ _____

☐ _____   ☐ _____

A SELF-CARE GOAL FOR TODAY:

_____

_____

A CHALLENGE I'M FACING: SOMETHING I'M EXCITED ABOUT:

_____   _____

_____   _____

_____   _____

HOW I SPENT MY TIME TODAY:

☐ MY LIFE'S PASSION   ☐ WORKING   ☐ TIME WITH FRIENDS/FAMILY

☐ VOLUNTEERING   ☐ SELF-CARE   ☐ TIME OUTDOORS

☐ ONLINE/SOCIAL MEDIA   ☐ DOWN TIME   ☐ OTHER:_____

EVENING REFLECTION

HOW I'M FEELING:

_____

_____

_____

THIS BROUGHT ME THE GREATEST JOY TODAY:

_____

_____

SOMETHING I DID TODAY THAT FELT MEANINGFUL:

_____

_____

_____

WHAT I DID TODAY THAT ALIGNED WITH MY PURPOSE:

_____

_____

_____

A NOTABLE RESULT FROM LIVING MY PURPOSE:

_____

_____

_____

A SETBACK I FACED TODAY AND HOW
I CAN LEARN OR GROW FROM THIS:

_____

_____

_____

MORNING REFLECTION

DATE ___/___/___

MY PURPOSE OR INTENTION FOR TODAY:

_____

_____

_____

GOALS ALIGNED WITH MY PURPOSE:

_____   _____

_____   _____

_____   _____

ACTION STEPS I CAN TAKE TODAY:

☐ _____   ☐ _____

☐ _____   ☐ _____

☐ _____   ☐ _____

A SELF-CARE GOAL FOR TODAY:

_____

_____

A CHALLENGE I'M FACING: SOMETHING I'M EXCITED ABOUT:

_____   _____

_____   _____

_____   _____

HOW I SPENT MY TIME TODAY:

☐ MY LIFE'S PASSION   ☐ WORKING   ☐ TIME WITH FRIENDS/FAMILY

☐ VOLUNTEERING   ☐ SELF-CARE   ☐ TIME OUTDOORS

☐ ONLINE/SOCIAL MEDIA   ☐ DOWN TIME   ☐ OTHER: _____

EVENING REFLECTION

HOW I'M FEELING:

_____

_____

_____

THIS BROUGHT ME THE GREATEST JOY TODAY:

_____

_____

SOMETHING I DID TODAY THAT FELT MEANINGFUL:

_____

_____

WHAT I DID TODAY THAT ALIGNED WITH MY PURPOSE:

_____

_____

A NOTABLE RESULT FROM LIVING MY PURPOSE:

_____

_____

A SETBACK I FACED TODAY AND HOW
I CAN LEARN OR GROW FROM THIS:

_____

_____

_____

MORNING REFLECTION

DATE ___/___/___

MY PURPOSE OR INTENTION FOR TODAY:

_____
_____
_____

GOALS ALIGNED WITH MY PURPOSE:

_____   _____
_____   _____
_____   _____

ACTION STEPS I CAN TAKE TODAY:

☐ _____   ☐ _____
☐ _____   ☐ _____
☐ _____   ☐

A SELF-CARE GOAL FOR TODAY:

_____
_____

A CHALLENGE I'M FACING: SOMETHING I'M EXCITED ABOUT:

_____   _____
_____   _____
_____   _____

HOW I SPENT MY TIME TODAY:

☐ MY LIFE'S PASSION   ☐ WORKING   ☐ TIME WITH FRIENDS/FAMILY
☐ VOLUNTEERING   ☐ SELF-CARE   ☐ TIME OUTDOORS
☐ ONLINE/SOCIAL MEDIA   ☐ DOWN TIME   ☐ OTHER:_____

EVENING REFLECTION

HOW I'M FEELING:

_____

_____

_____

THIS BROUGHT ME THE GREATEST JOY TODAY:

_____

_____

SOMETHING I DID TODAY THAT FELT MEANINGFUL:

_____

_____

_____

WHAT I DID TODAY THAT ALIGNED WITH MY PURPOSE:

_____

_____

_____

A NOTABLE RESULT FROM LIVING MY PURPOSE:

_____

_____

_____

A SETBACK I FACED TODAY AND HOW
I CAN LEARN OR GROW FROM THIS:

_____

_____

_____

_____

MORNING REFLECTION

DATE ___/___/___

MY PURPOSE OR INTENTION FOR TODAY:

_____
_____
_____

GOALS ALIGNED WITH MY PURPOSE:

_____   _____
_____   _____
_____   _____

ACTION STEPS I CAN TAKE TODAY:

☐ _____   ☐ _____
☐ _____   ☐ _____
☐ _____   ☐ _____

A SELF-CARE GOAL FOR TODAY:

_____
_____

A CHALLENGE I'M FACING: SOMETHING I'M EXCITED ABOUT:

_____   _____
_____   _____
_____   _____

HOW I SPENT MY TIME TODAY:

☐ MY LIFE'S PASSION   ☐ WORKING   ☐ TIME WITH FRIENDS/FAMILY
☐ VOLUNTEERING   ☐ SELF-CARE   ☐ TIME OUTDOORS
☐ ONLINE/SOCIAL MEDIA   ☐ DOWN TIME   ☐ OTHER: _____

EVENING REFLECTION

HOW I'M FEELING:

_____

_____

_____

THIS BROUGHT ME THE GREATEST JOY TODAY:

_____

_____

SOMETHING I DID TODAY THAT FELT MEANINGFUL:

_____

_____

_____

WHAT I DID TODAY THAT ALIGNED WITH MY PURPOSE:

_____

_____

_____

A NOTABLE RESULT FROM LIVING MY PURPOSE:

_____

_____

_____

A SETBACK I FACED TODAY AND HOW
I CAN LEARN OR GROW FROM THIS:

_____

_____

_____

_____

MORNING REFLECTION

DATE ___/___/___

MY PURPOSE OR INTENTION FOR TODAY:

_____

_____

_____

GOALS ALIGNED WITH MY PURPOSE:

_____   _____

_____   _____

_____   _____

ACTION STEPS I CAN TAKE TODAY:

☐ _____   ☐ _____

☐ _____   ☐ _____

☐ _____   ☐ _____

A SELF-CARE GOAL FOR TODAY:

_____

_____

A CHALLENGE I'M FACING: SOMETHING I'M EXCITED ABOUT:

_____   _____

_____   _____

HOW I SPENT MY TIME TODAY:

☐ MY LIFE'S PASSION   ☐ WORKING   ☐ TIME WITH FRIENDS/FAMILY

☐ VOLUNTEERING   ☐ SELF-CARE   ☐ TIME OUTDOORS

☐ ONLINE/SOCIAL MEDIA   ☐ DOWN TIME   ☐ OTHER: _____

EVENING REFLECTION

HOW I'M FEELING:

_____

_____

_____

THIS BROUGHT ME THE GREATEST JOY TODAY:

_____

_____

SOMETHING I DID TODAY THAT FELT MEANINGFUL:

_____

_____

_____

WHAT I DID TODAY THAT ALIGNED WITH MY PURPOSE:

_____

_____

_____

A NOTABLE RESULT FROM LIVING MY PURPOSE:

_____

_____

_____

A SETBACK I FACED TODAY AND HOW
I CAN LEARN OR GROW FROM THIS:

_____

_____

_____

MORNING REFLECTION

DATE ___/___/___

MY PURPOSE OR INTENTION FOR TODAY:

_____
_____
_____

GOALS ALIGNED WITH MY PURPOSE:

_____   _____
_____   _____
_____   _____

ACTION STEPS I CAN TAKE TODAY:

☐ _____   ☐ _____
☐ _____   ☐ _____
☐ _____   ☐ _____

A SELF-CARE GOAL FOR TODAY:

_____
_____

A CHALLENGE I'M FACING: SOMETHING I'M EXCITED ABOUT:

_____   _____
_____   _____
_____   _____

HOW I SPENT MY TIME TODAY:

☐ MY LIFE'S PASSION   ☐ WORKING   ☐ TIME WITH FRIENDS/FAMILY
☐ VOLUNTEERING   ☐ SELF-CARE   ☐ TIME OUTDOORS
☐ ONLINE/SOCIAL MEDIA   ☐ DOWN TIME   ☐ OTHER: _____

EVENING REFLECTION

HOW I'M FEELING:

_____

_____

_____

THIS BROUGHT ME THE GREATEST JOY TODAY:

_____

_____

SOMETHING I DID TODAY THAT FELT MEANINGFUL:

_____

_____

_____

WHAT I DID TODAY THAT ALIGNED WITH MY PURPOSE:

_____

_____

_____

A NOTABLE RESULT FROM LIVING MY PURPOSE:

_____

_____

_____

A SETBACK I FACED TODAY AND HOW
I CAN LEARN OR GROW FROM THIS:

_____

_____

_____

_____

MORNING REFLECTION

DATE ___/___/___

MY PURPOSE OR INTENTION FOR TODAY:
_____
_____
_____

GOALS ALIGNED WITH MY PURPOSE:
_____   _____
_____   _____
_____

ACTION STEPS I CAN TAKE TODAY:

☐ _____   ☐ _____
☐ _____   ☐ _____
☐ _____   ☐ _____

A SELF-CARE GOAL FOR TODAY:
_____
_____

A CHALLENGE I'M FACING: SOMETHING I'M EXCITED ABOUT:
_____   _____
_____   _____

HOW I SPENT MY TIME TODAY:

☐ MY LIFE'S PASSION   ☐ WORKING   ☐ TIME WITH FRIENDS/FAMILY
☐ VOLUNTEERING   ☐ SELF-CARE   ☐ TIME OUTDOORS
☐ ONLINE/SOCIAL MEDIA   ☐ DOWN TIME   ☐ OTHER: _____

EVENING REFLECTION

HOW I'M FEELING:

_____

_____

_____

THIS BROUGHT ME THE GREATEST JOY TODAY:

_____

_____

SOMETHING I DID TODAY THAT FELT MEANINGFUL:

_____

_____

_____

WHAT I DID TODAY THAT ALIGNED WITH MY PURPOSE:

_____

_____

_____

A NOTABLE RESULT FROM LIVING MY PURPOSE:

_____

_____

_____

A SETBACK I FACED TODAY AND HOW
I CAN LEARN OR GROW FROM THIS:

_____

_____

_____

_____

MORNING REFLECTION

DATE ___/___/___

MY PURPOSE OR INTENTION FOR TODAY:

_____

_____

_____

GOALS ALIGNED WITH MY PURPOSE:

_____   _____

_____   _____

_____   _____

ACTION STEPS I CAN TAKE TODAY:

☐ _____   ☐ _____

☐ _____   ☐ _____

☐ _____   ☐ _____

A SELF-CARE GOAL FOR TODAY:

_____

_____

A CHALLENGE I'M FACING: SOMETHING I'M EXCITED ABOUT:

_____   _____

_____   _____

_____   _____

HOW I SPENT MY TIME TODAY:

☐ MY LIFE'S PASSION   ☐ WORKING   ☐ TIME WITH FRIENDS/FAMILY

☐ VOLUNTEERING   ☐ SELF-CARE   ☐ TIME OUTDOORS

☐ ONLINE/SOCIAL MEDIA   ☐ DOWN TIME   ☐ OTHER: _____

EVENING REFLECTION

HOW I'M FEELING:
_____
_____
_____

THIS BROUGHT ME THE GREATEST JOY TODAY:
_____
_____

SOMETHING I DID TODAY THAT FELT MEANINGFUL:
_____
_____
_____

WHAT I DID TODAY THAT ALIGNED WITH MY PURPOSE:
_____
_____
_____

A NOTABLE RESULT FROM LIVING MY PURPOSE:
_____
_____
_____

A SETBACK I FACED TODAY AND HOW
I CAN LEARN OR GROW FROM THIS:
_____
_____
_____
_____

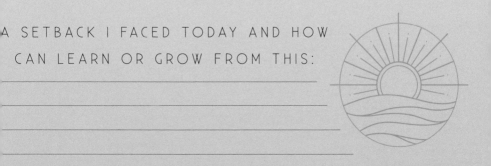

MORNING REFLECTION

DATE ___ / ___ / __

MY PURPOSE OR INTENTION FOR TODAY:

_____

_____

_____

GOALS ALIGNED WITH MY PURPOSE:

_____   _____

_____   _____

_____   _____

ACTION STEPS I CAN TAKE TODAY:

☐ _____   ☐ _____

☐ _____   ☐ _____

☐ _____   ☐ _____

A SELF-CARE GOAL FOR TODAY:

_____

_____

A CHALLENGE I'M FACING: SOMETHING I'M EXCITED ABOUT:

_____   _____

_____   _____

_____   _____

HOW I SPENT MY TIME TODAY:

☐ MY LIFE'S PASSION   ☐ WORKING   ☐ TIME WITH FRIENDS/FAMILY

☐ VOLUNTEERING   ☐ SELF-CARE   ☐ TIME OUTDOORS

☐ ONLINE/SOCIAL MEDIA   ☐ DOWN TIME   ☐ OTHER: _____

EVENING REFLECTION

HOW I'M FEELING:

_____
_____
_____

THIS BROUGHT ME THE GREATEST JOY TODAY:

_____
_____

SOMETHING I DID TODAY THAT FELT MEANINGFUL:

_____
_____
_____

WHAT I DID TODAY THAT ALIGNED WITH MY PURPOSE:

_____
_____
_____

A NOTABLE RESULT FROM LIVING MY PURPOSE:

_____
_____
_____

A SETBACK I FACED TODAY AND HOW
I CAN LEARN OR GROW FROM THIS:

_____
_____

_____
_____

MORNING REFLECTION

DATE ___ / ___ / ___

MY PURPOSE OR INTENTION FOR TODAY:

_____

_____

_____

GOALS ALIGNED WITH MY PURPOSE:

_____   _____

_____   _____

_____   _____

ACTION STEPS I CAN TAKE TODAY:

☐ _____   ☐ _____

☐ _____   ☐ _____

☐ _____   ☐ _____

A SELF-CARE GOAL FOR TODAY:

_____

_____

A CHALLENGE I'M FACING:

_____

_____

_____

SOMETHING I'M EXCITED ABOUT:

_____

_____

_____

HOW I SPENT MY TIME TODAY:

☐ MY LIFE'S PASSION   ☐ WORKING   ☐ TIME WITH FRIENDS/FAMILY

☐ VOLUNTEERING   ☐ SELF-CARE   ☐ TIME OUTDOORS

☐ ONLINE/SOCIAL MEDIA   ☐ DOWN TIME   ☐ OTHER: _____

EVENING REFLECTION

HOW I'M FEELING:

_____
_____
_____

THIS BROUGHT ME THE GREATEST JOY TODAY:

_____
_____

SOMETHING I DID TODAY THAT FELT MEANINGFUL:

_____
_____
_____

WHAT I DID TODAY THAT ALIGNED WITH MY PURPOSE:

_____
_____
_____

A NOTABLE RESULT FROM LIVING MY PURPOSE:

_____
_____
_____

A SETBACK I FACED TODAY AND HOW
I CAN LEARN OR GROW FROM THIS:

_____
_____
_____

_____

MORNING REFLECTION

DATE ___/___/___

MY PURPOSE OR INTENTION FOR TODAY:

_____

_____

_____

GOALS ALIGNED WITH MY PURPOSE:

_____   _____

_____   _____

_____   _____

ACTION STEPS I CAN TAKE TODAY:

☐ _____   ☐ _____

☐ _____   ☐ _____

☐ _____   ☐ _____

A SELF-CARE GOAL FOR TODAY:

_____

_____

A CHALLENGE I'M FACING:

_____

_____

_____

SOMETHING I'M EXCITED ABOUT:

_____

_____

_____

HOW I SPENT MY TIME TODAY:

☐ MY LIFE'S PASSION   ☐ WORKING   ☐ TIME WITH FRIENDS/FAMILY

☐ VOLUNTEERING   ☐ SELF-CARE   ☐ TIME OUTDOORS

☐ ONLINE/SOCIAL MEDIA   ☐ DOWN TIME   ☐ OTHER: _____

EVENING REFLECTION

HOW I'M FEELING:

_____

_____

_____

THIS BROUGHT ME THE GREATEST JOY TODAY:

_____

_____

SOMETHING I DID TODAY THAT FELT MEANINGFUL:

_____

_____

_____

WHAT I DID TODAY THAT ALIGNED WITH MY PURPOSE:

_____

_____

_____

A NOTABLE RESULT FROM LIVING MY PURPOSE:

_____

_____

_____

A SETBACK I FACED TODAY AND HOW
I CAN LEARN OR GROW FROM THIS:

_____

_____

_____

MORNING REFLECTION

DATE ___/___/___

MY PURPOSE OR INTENTION FOR TODAY:

_____
_____
_____

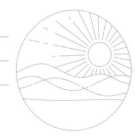

GOALS ALIGNED WITH MY PURPOSE:

_____   _____
_____   _____
_____   _____

ACTION STEPS I CAN TAKE TODAY:

☐ _____   ☐ _____
☐ _____   ☐ _____
☐ _____   ☐ _____

A SELF-CARE GOAL FOR TODAY:

_____
_____

A CHALLENGE I'M FACING: SOMETHING I'M EXCITED ABOUT:

_____   _____
_____   _____
_____   _____

HOW I SPENT MY TIME TODAY:

☐ MY LIFE'S PASSION   ☐ WORKING   ☐ TIME WITH FRIENDS/FAMILY
☐ VOLUNTEERING   ☐ SELF-CARE   ☐ TIME OUTDOORS
☐ ONLINE/SOCIAL MEDIA   ☐ DOWN TIME   ☐ OTHER: _____

EVENING REFLECTION

HOW I'M FEELING:
_____
_____
_____

THIS BROUGHT ME THE GREATEST JOY TODAY:
_____
_____

SOMETHING I DID TODAY THAT FELT MEANINGFUL:
_____
_____
_____

WHAT I DID TODAY THAT ALIGNED WITH MY PURPOSE:
_____
_____
_____

A NOTABLE RESULT FROM LIVING MY PURPOSE:
_____
_____
_____

A SETBACK I FACED TODAY AND HOW
I CAN LEARN OR GROW FROM THIS:
_____
_____
_____
_____

MORNING REFLECTION

DATE ___ / ___ / ___

MY PURPOSE OR INTENTION FOR TODAY:

_____

_____

_____

GOALS ALIGNED WITH MY PURPOSE:

_____   _____

_____   _____

_____   _____

ACTION STEPS I CAN TAKE TODAY:

☐ _____   ☐ _____

☐ _____   ☐ _____

☐ _____   ☐ _____

A SELF-CARE GOAL FOR TODAY:

_____

_____

A CHALLENGE I'M FACING: SOMETHING I'M EXCITED ABOUT:

_____   _____

_____   _____

_____   _____

HOW I SPENT MY TIME TODAY:

☐ MY LIFE'S PASSION   ☐ WORKING   ☐ TIME WITH FRIENDS/FAMILY

☐ VOLUNTEERING   ☐ SELF-CARE   ☐ TIME OUTDOORS

☐ ONLINE/SOCIAL MEDIA   ☐ DOWN TIME   ☐ OTHER: _____

EVENING REFLECTION

HOW I'M FEELING:

_____

_____

_____

THIS BROUGHT ME THE GREATEST JOY TODAY:

_____

_____

SOMETHING I DID TODAY THAT FELT MEANINGFUL:

_____

_____

_____

WHAT I DID TODAY THAT ALIGNED WITH MY PURPOSE:

_____

_____

_____

A NOTABLE RESULT FROM LIVING MY PURPOSE:

_____

_____

_____

A SETBACK I FACED TODAY AND HOW
I CAN LEARN OR GROW FROM THIS:

_____

_____

_____

MORNING REFLECTION

MY PURPOSE OR INTENTION FOR TODAY:

_____

_____

_____

GOALS ALIGNED WITH MY PURPOSE:

_____   _____

_____   _____

_____   _____

ACTION STEPS I CAN TAKE TODAY:

☐ _____   ☐ _____

☐ _____   ☐ _____

☐ _____   ☐ _____

A SELF-CARE GOAL FOR TODAY:

_____

_____

A CHALLENGE I'M FACING:

_____

_____

_____

SOMETHING I'M EXCITED ABOUT:

_____

_____

_____

HOW I SPENT MY TIME TODAY:

☐ MY LIFE'S PASSION   ☐ WORKING   ☐ TIME WITH FRIENDS/FAMILY

☐ VOLUNTEERING   ☐ SELF-CARE   ☐ TIME OUTDOORS

☐ ONLINE/SOCIAL MEDIA   ☐ DOWN TIME   ☐ OTHER: _____

EVENING REFLECTION

HOW I'M FEELING:

_____

_____

_____

THIS BROUGHT ME THE GREATEST JOY TODAY:

_____

_____

SOMETHING I DID TODAY THAT FELT MEANINGFUL:

_____

_____

_____

WHAT I DID TODAY THAT ALIGNED WITH MY PURPOSE:

_____

_____

_____

A NOTABLE RESULT FROM LIVING MY PURPOSE:

_____

_____

_____

A SETBACK I FACED TODAY AND HOW
I CAN LEARN OR GROW FROM THIS:

_____

_____

_____

_____

MORNING REFLECTION

DATE ___ / ___ / ___

MY PURPOSE OR INTENTION FOR TODAY:

_____

_____

_____

GOALS ALIGNED WITH MY PURPOSE:

_____   _____

_____   _____

_____   _____

ACTION STEPS I CAN TAKE TODAY:

☐ _____   ☐ _____

☐ _____   ☐ _____

☐ _____   ☐ _____

A SELF-CARE GOAL FOR TODAY:

_____

_____

A CHALLENGE I'M FACING: ## SOMETHING I'M EXCITED ABOUT:

_____   _____

_____   _____

_____   _____

HOW I SPENT MY TIME TODAY:

☐ MY LIFE'S PASSION   ☐ WORKING   ☐ TIME WITH FRIENDS/FAMILY

☐ VOLUNTEERING   ☐ SELF-CARE   ☐ TIME OUTDOORS

☐ ONLINE/SOCIAL MEDIA   ☐ DOWN TIME   ☐ OTHER: _____

EVENING REFLECTION

HOW I'M FEELING:

_____

_____

_____

THIS BROUGHT ME THE GREATEST JOY TODAY:

_____

_____

SOMETHING I DID TODAY THAT FELT MEANINGFUL:

_____

_____

_____

WHAT I DID TODAY THAT ALIGNED WITH MY PURPOSE:

_____

_____

_____

A NOTABLE RESULT FROM LIVING MY PURPOSE:

_____

_____

_____

A SETBACK I FACED TODAY AND HOW
I CAN LEARN OR GROW FROM THIS:

_____

_____

_____

_____

MORNING REFLECTION

DATE ___/___/___

MY PURPOSE OR INTENTION FOR TODAY:
_____
_____
_____

GOALS ALIGNED WITH MY PURPOSE:
_____   _____
_____   _____
_____   _____

ACTION STEPS I CAN TAKE TODAY:
☐ _____   ☐ _____
☐ _____   ☐ _____
☐ _____   ☐ _____

A SELF-CARE GOAL FOR TODAY:
_____
_____

A CHALLENGE I'M FACING: SOMETHING I'M EXCITED ABOUT:
_____   _____
_____   _____
_____   _____

HOW I SPENT MY TIME TODAY:

☐ MY LIFE'S PASSION   ☐ WORKING   ☐ TIME WITH FRIENDS/FAMILY
☐ VOLUNTEERING   ☐ SELF-CARE   ☐ TIME OUTDOORS
☐ ONLINE/SOCIAL MEDIA   ☐ DOWN TIME   ☐ OTHER: _____

EVENING REFLECTION

HOW I'M FEELING:

_____

_____

_____

THIS BROUGHT ME THE GREATEST JOY TODAY:

_____

_____

SOMETHING I DID TODAY THAT FELT MEANINGFUL:

_____

_____

_____

WHAT I DID TODAY THAT ALIGNED WITH MY PURPOSE:

_____

_____

_____

A NOTABLE RESULT FROM LIVING MY PURPOSE:

_____

_____

_____

A SETBACK I FACED TODAY AND HOW
I CAN LEARN OR GROW FROM THIS:

_____

_____

_____

_____

MORNING REFLECTION

DATE ___/___/___

MY PURPOSE OR INTENTION FOR TODAY:

_____

_____

_____

GOALS ALIGNED WITH MY PURPOSE:

_____   _____

_____   _____

_____   _____

ACTION STEPS I CAN TAKE TODAY:

☐ _____   ☐ _____

☐ _____   ☐ _____

☐ _____   ☐ _____

A SELF-CARE GOAL FOR TODAY:

_____

_____

A CHALLENGE I'M FACING:

_____

_____

_____

SOMETHING I'M EXCITED ABOUT:

_____

_____

_____

HOW I SPENT MY TIME TODAY:

☐ MY LIFE'S PASSION   ☐ WORKING   ☐ TIME WITH FRIENDS/FAMILY

☐ VOLUNTEERING   ☐ SELF-CARE   ☐ TIME OUTDOORS

☐ ONLINE/SOCIAL MEDIA   ☐ DOWN TIME   ☐ OTHER: _____

EVENING REFLECTION

HOW I'M FEELING:

_____
_____
_____

THIS BROUGHT ME THE GREATEST JOY TODAY:

_____
_____

SOMETHING I DID TODAY THAT FELT MEANINGFUL:

_____
_____
_____

WHAT I DID TODAY THAT ALIGNED WITH MY PURPOSE:

_____
_____
_____

A NOTABLE RESULT FROM LIVING MY PURPOSE:

_____
_____
_____

A SETBACK I FACED TODAY AND HOW
I CAN LEARN OR GROW FROM THIS:

_____
_____
_____

MORNING REFLECTION

DATE ___/___/___

MY PURPOSE OR INTENTION FOR TODAY:
_____
_____
_____

GOALS ALIGNED WITH MY PURPOSE:
_____   _____
_____   _____
_____   _____

ACTION STEPS I CAN TAKE TODAY:

☐ _____   ☐ _____
☐ _____   ☐ _____
☐ _____   ☐ _____

A SELF-CARE GOAL FOR TODAY:
_____
_____

A CHALLENGE I'M FACING: SOMETHING I'M EXCITED ABOUT:
_____   _____
_____   _____

HOW I SPENT MY TIME TODAY:

☐ MY LIFE'S PASSION   ☐ WORKING   ☐ TIME WITH FRIENDS/FAMILY
☐ VOLUNTEERING   ☐ SELF-CARE   ☐ TIME OUTDOORS
☐ ONLINE/SOCIAL MEDIA   ☐ DOWN TIME   ☐ OTHER: _____

EVENING REFLECTION

HOW I'M FEELING:

_____

_____

_____

THIS BROUGHT ME THE GREATEST JOY TODAY:

_____

_____

SOMETHING I DID TODAY THAT FELT MEANINGFUL:

_____

_____

_____

WHAT I DID TODAY THAT ALIGNED WITH MY PURPOSE:

_____

_____

_____

A NOTABLE RESULT FROM LIVING MY PURPOSE:

_____

_____

_____

A SETBACK I FACED TODAY AND HOW
I CAN LEARN OR GROW FROM THIS:

_____

_____

_____

_____

MORNING REFLECTION

DATE ____ / ____ / ____

MY PURPOSE OR INTENTION FOR TODAY:

_____

_____

_____

GOALS ALIGNED WITH MY PURPOSE:

_____   _____

_____   _____

_____   _____

ACTION STEPS I CAN TAKE TODAY:

☐ _____   ☐ _____

☐ _____   ☐ _____

☐ _____   ☐ _____

A SELF-CARE GOAL FOR TODAY:

_____

_____

A CHALLENGE I'M FACING:

_____

_____

_____

SOMETHING I'M EXCITED ABOUT:

_____

_____

_____

HOW I SPENT MY TIME TODAY:

☐ MY LIFE'S PASSION   ☐ WORKING   ☐ TIME WITH FRIENDS/FAMILY

☐ VOLUNTEERING   ☐ SELF-CARE   ☐ TIME OUTDOORS

☐ ONLINE/SOCIAL MEDIA   ☐ DOWN TIME   ☐ OTHER: _____

EVENING REFLECTION

HOW I'M FEELING:

_____

_____

_____

THIS BROUGHT ME THE GREATEST JOY TODAY:

_____

_____

SOMETHING I DID TODAY THAT FELT MEANINGFUL:

_____

_____

_____

WHAT I DID TODAY THAT ALIGNED WITH MY PURPOSE:

_____

_____

_____

A NOTABLE RESULT FROM LIVING MY PURPOSE:

_____

_____

_____

A SETBACK I FACED TODAY AND HOW
I CAN LEARN OR GROW FROM THIS:

_____

_____

_____

_____

MORNING REFLECTION

DATE ___ / ___ /___

MY PURPOSE OR INTENTION FOR TODAY:

_____

_____

_____

GOALS ALIGNED WITH MY PURPOSE:

_____   _____

_____   _____

_____   _____

ACTION STEPS I CAN TAKE TODAY:

☐ _____   ☐ _____

☐ _____   ☐ _____

☐ _____   ☐ _____

A SELF-CARE GOAL FOR TODAY:

_____

_____

A CHALLENGE I'M FACING: SOMETHING I'M EXCITED ABOUT:

_____   _____

_____   _____

_____   _____

HOW I SPENT MY TIME TODAY:

☐ MY LIFE'S PASSION   ☐ WORKING   ☐ TIME WITH FRIENDS/FAMILY

☐ VOLUNTEERING   ☐ SELF-CARE   ☐ TIME OUTDOORS

☐ ONLINE/SOCIAL MEDIA   ☐ DOWN TIME   ☐ OTHER: _____

EVENING REFLECTION

HOW I'M FEELING:

_____

_____

_____

THIS BROUGHT ME THE GREATEST JOY TODAY:

_____

_____

SOMETHING I DID TODAY THAT FELT MEANINGFUL:

_____

_____

_____

WHAT I DID TODAY THAT ALIGNED WITH MY PURPOSE:

_____

_____

_____

A NOTABLE RESULT FROM LIVING MY PURPOSE:

_____

_____

_____

A SETBACK I FACED TODAY AND HOW
I CAN LEARN OR GROW FROM THIS:

_____

_____

_____

MORNING REFLECTION

DATE ___ / ___ / ___

MY PURPOSE OR INTENTION FOR TODAY:

_____

_____

_____

GOALS ALIGNED WITH MY PURPOSE:

_____   _____

_____   _____

_____   _____

ACTION STEPS I CAN TAKE TODAY:

☐ _____   ☐ _____

☐ _____   ☐ _____

☐ _____   ☐ _____

A SELF-CARE GOAL FOR TODAY:

_____

_____

A CHALLENGE I'M FACING: SOMETHING I'M EXCITED ABOUT:

_____   _____

_____   _____

HOW I SPENT MY TIME TODAY:

☐ MY LIFE'S PASSION   ☐ WORKING   ☐ TIME WITH FRIENDS/FAMILY

☐ VOLUNTEERING   ☐ SELF-CARE   ☐ TIME OUTDOORS

☐ ONLINE/SOCIAL MEDIA   ☐ DOWN TIME   ☐ OTHER: _____

EVENING REFLECTION

HOW I'M FEELING:

_____

_____

_____

THIS BROUGHT ME THE GREATEST JOY TODAY:

_____

_____

SOMETHING I DID TODAY THAT FELT MEANINGFUL:

_____

_____

_____

WHAT I DID TODAY THAT ALIGNED WITH MY PURPOSE:

_____

_____

_____

A NOTABLE RESULT FROM LIVING MY PURPOSE:

_____

_____

_____

A SETBACK I FACED TODAY AND HOW
I CAN LEARN OR GROW FROM THIS:

_____

_____

_____

MORNING REFLECTION

DATE ___ / ___ / ___

MY PURPOSE OR INTENTION FOR TODAY:

_____

_____

_____

GOALS ALIGNED WITH MY PURPOSE:

_____ _____

_____ _____

_____ _____

ACTION STEPS I CAN TAKE TODAY:

☐ _____ ☐ _____

☐ _____ ☐ _____

☐ _____ ☐ _____

A SELF-CARE GOAL FOR TODAY:

_____

_____

A CHALLENGE I'M FACING: SOMETHING I'M EXCITED ABOUT:

_____ _____

_____ _____

_____ _____

HOW I SPENT MY TIME TODAY:

☐ MY LIFE'S PASSION   ☐ WORKING   ☐ TIME WITH FRIENDS/FAMILY

☐ VOLUNTEERING   ☐ SELF-CARE   ☐ TIME OUTDOORS

☐ ONLINE/SOCIAL MEDIA   ☐ DOWN TIME   ☐ OTHER: _____

EVENING REFLECTION

HOW I'M FEELING:

_____
_____
_____

THIS BROUGHT ME THE GREATEST JOY TODAY:

_____
_____

SOMETHING I DID TODAY THAT FELT MEANINGFUL:

_____
_____
_____

WHAT I DID TODAY THAT ALIGNED WITH MY PURPOSE:

_____
_____
_____

A NOTABLE RESULT FROM LIVING MY PURPOSE:

_____
_____
_____

A SETBACK I FACED TODAY AND HOW
I CAN LEARN OR GROW FROM THIS:

_____
_____
_____
_____

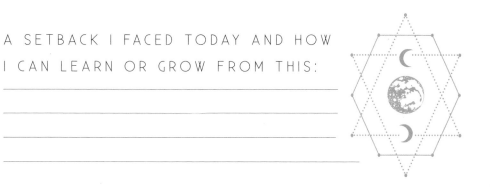

MORNING REFLECTION

DATE ___ / ___ / ___

MY PURPOSE OR INTENTION FOR TODAY:

_____

_____

_____

GOALS ALIGNED WITH MY PURPOSE:

_____   _____

_____   _____

_____   _____

ACTION STEPS I CAN TAKE TODAY:

☐ _____   ☐ _____

☐ _____   ☐ _____

☐ _____   ☐ _____

A SELF-CARE GOAL FOR TODAY:

_____

_____

A CHALLENGE I'M FACING: SOMETHING I'M EXCITED ABOUT:

_____   _____

_____   _____

_____   _____

HOW I SPENT MY TIME TODAY:

☐ MY LIFE'S PASSION   ☐ WORKING   ☐ TIME WITH FRIENDS/FAMILY

☐ VOLUNTEERING   ☐ SELF-CARE   ☐ TIME OUTDOORS

☐ ONLINE/SOCIAL MEDIA   ☐ DOWN TIME   ☐ OTHER: _____

EVENING REFLECTION

HOW I'M FEELING:

_____

_____

_____

THIS BROUGHT ME THE GREATEST JOY TODAY:

_____

_____

SOMETHING I DID TODAY THAT FELT MEANINGFUL:

_____

_____

_____

WHAT I DID TODAY THAT ALIGNED WITH MY PURPOSE:

_____

_____

_____

A NOTABLE RESULT FROM LIVING MY PURPOSE:

_____

_____

_____

A SETBACK I FACED TODAY AND HOW
I CAN LEARN OR GROW FROM THIS:

_____

_____

_____

_____

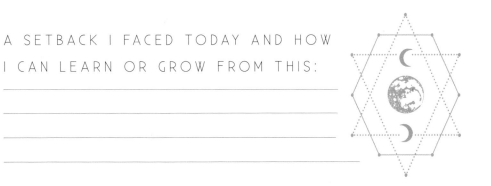

MORNING REFLECTION

DATE ___ / ___ / ___

MY PURPOSE OR INTENTION FOR TODAY:

_____

_____

_____

GOALS ALIGNED WITH MY PURPOSE:

_____   _____

_____   _____

_____   _____

ACTION STEPS I CAN TAKE TODAY:

☐ _____   ☐ _____

☐ _____   ☐ _____

☐ _____   ☐ _____

A SELF-CARE GOAL FOR TODAY:

_____

_____

A CHALLENGE I'M FACING: SOMETHING I'M EXCITED ABOUT:

_____   _____

_____   _____

_____   _____

HOW I SPENT MY TIME TODAY:

☐ MY LIFE'S PASSION   ☐ WORKING   ☐ TIME WITH FRIENDS/FAMILY

☐ VOLUNTEERING   ☐ SELF-CARE   ☐ TIME OUTDOORS

☐ ONLINE/SOCIAL MEDIA   ☐ DOWN TIME   ☐ OTHER: _____

EVENING REFLECTION

HOW I'M FEELING:

_____

_____

_____

THIS BROUGHT ME THE GREATEST JOY TODAY:

_____

_____

SOMETHING I DID TODAY THAT FELT MEANINGFUL:

_____

_____

_____

WHAT I DID TODAY THAT ALIGNED WITH MY PURPOSE:

_____

_____

_____

A NOTABLE RESULT FROM LIVING MY PURPOSE:

_____

_____

_____

A SETBACK I FACED TODAY AND HOW
I CAN LEARN OR GROW FROM THIS:

_____

_____

_____

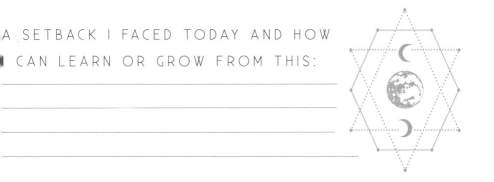

MORNING REFLECTION

DATE ___ / ___ / ___

MY PURPOSE OR INTENTION FOR TODAY:

_____
_____
_____

GOALS ALIGNED WITH MY PURPOSE:

_____   _____
_____   _____
_____   _____

ACTION STEPS I CAN TAKE TODAY:

☐ _____   ☐ _____
☐ _____   ☐ _____
☐ _____   ☐ _____

A SELF-CARE GOAL FOR TODAY:

_____
_____

A CHALLENGE I'M FACING: SOMETHING I'M EXCITED ABOUT:

_____   _____
_____   _____
_____   _____

HOW I SPENT MY TIME TODAY:

☐ MY LIFE'S PASSION   ☐ WORKING   ☐ TIME WITH FRIENDS/FAMILY
☐ VOLUNTEERING   ☐ SELF-CARE   ☐ TIME OUTDOORS
☐ ONLINE/SOCIAL MEDIA   ☐ DOWN TIME   ☐ OTHER: _____

EVENING REFLECTION

HOW I'M FEELING:

_____
_____
_____

THIS BROUGHT ME THE GREATEST JOY TODAY:

_____
_____

SOMETHING I DID TODAY THAT FELT MEANINGFUL:

_____
_____
_____

WHAT I DID TODAY THAT ALIGNED WITH MY PURPOSE:

_____
_____
_____

A NOTABLE RESULT FROM LIVING MY PURPOSE:

_____
_____
_____

A SETBACK I FACED TODAY AND HOW
I CAN LEARN OR GROW FROM THIS:

_____
_____
_____

MORNING REFLECTION

DATE ___ / ___ / ___

MY PURPOSE OR INTENTION FOR TODAY:

_____
_____
_____

GOALS ALIGNED WITH MY PURPOSE:

_____   _____
_____   _____
_____   _____

ACTION STEPS I CAN TAKE TODAY:

☐ _____   ☐ _____
☐ _____   ☐ _____
☐ _____   ☐ _____

A SELF-CARE GOAL FOR TODAY:

_____
_____

A CHALLENGE I'M FACING: SOMETHING I'M EXCITED ABOUT:

_____   _____
_____   _____
_____   _____

HOW I SPENT MY TIME TODAY:

☐ MY LIFE'S PASSION   ☐ WORKING   ☐ TIME WITH FRIENDS/FAMILY
☐ VOLUNTEERING   ☐ SELF-CARE   ☐ TIME OUTDOORS
☐ ONLINE/SOCIAL MEDIA   ☐ DOWN TIME   ☐ OTHER: _____

EVENING REFLECTION

HOW I'M FEELING:

_____

_____

_____

THIS BROUGHT ME THE GREATEST JOY TODAY:

_____

_____

SOMETHING I DID TODAY THAT FELT MEANINGFUL:

_____

_____

_____

WHAT I DID TODAY THAT ALIGNED WITH MY PURPOSE:

_____

_____

_____

A NOTABLE RESULT FROM LIVING MY PURPOSE:

_____

_____

_____

A SETBACK I FACED TODAY AND HOW
I CAN LEARN OR GROW FROM THIS:

_____

_____

_____

MORNING REFLECTION

DATE ___ / ___ /

MY PURPOSE OR INTENTION FOR TODAY:

_____

_____

_____

GOALS ALIGNED WITH MY PURPOSE:

_____   _____

_____   _____

_____   _____

ACTION STEPS I CAN TAKE TODAY:

☐ _____   ☐ _____

☐ _____   ☐ _____

☐ _____   ☐ _____

A SELF-CARE GOAL FOR TODAY:

_____

_____

A CHALLENGE I'M FACING: SOMETHING I'M EXCITED ABOUT:

_____   _____

_____   _____

_____   _____

HOW I SPENT MY TIME TODAY:

☐ MY LIFE'S PASSION   ☐ WORKING   ☐ TIME WITH FRIENDS/FAMILY

☐ VOLUNTEERING   ☐ SELF-CARE   ☐ TIME OUTDOORS

☐ ONLINE/SOCIAL MEDIA   ☐ DOWN TIME   ☐ OTHER: _____

EVENING REFLECTION

HOW I'M FEELING:

_____

_____

_____

THIS BROUGHT ME THE GREATEST JOY TODAY:

_____

_____

SOMETHING I DID TODAY THAT FELT MEANINGFUL:

_____

_____

_____

WHAT I DID TODAY THAT ALIGNED WITH MY PURPOSE:

_____

_____

_____

A NOTABLE RESULT FROM LIVING MY PURPOSE:

_____

_____

_____

A SETBACK I FACED TODAY AND HOW
I CAN LEARN OR GROW FROM THIS:

_____

_____

_____

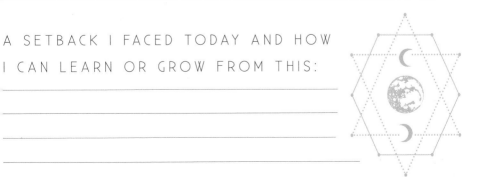

MORNING REFLECTION

DATE ___ / ___ / ___

MY PURPOSE OR INTENTION FOR TODAY:

_____

_____

_____

GOALS ALIGNED WITH MY PURPOSE:

_____   _____

_____   _____

_____   _____

ACTION STEPS I CAN TAKE TODAY:

☐ _____   ☐ _____

☐ _____   ☐ _____

☐ _____   ☐ _____

A SELF-CARE GOAL FOR TODAY:

_____

_____

A CHALLENGE I'M FACING: SOMETHING I'M EXCITED ABOUT:

_____   _____

_____   _____

_____   _____

HOW I SPENT MY TIME TODAY:

☐ MY LIFE'S PASSION   ☐ WORKING   ☐ TIME WITH FRIENDS/FAMILY

☐ VOLUNTEERING   ☐ SELF-CARE   ☐ TIME OUTDOORS

☐ ONLINE/SOCIAL MEDIA   ☐ DOWN TIME   ☐ OTHER: _____

EVENING REFLECTION

HOW I'M FEELING:

_____
_____
_____

THIS BROUGHT ME THE GREATEST JOY TODAY:

_____
_____

SOMETHING I DID TODAY THAT FELT MEANINGFUL:

_____
_____

WHAT I DID TODAY THAT ALIGNED WITH MY PURPOSE:

_____
_____
_____

A NOTABLE RESULT FROM LIVING MY PURPOSE:

_____
_____
_____

A SETBACK I FACED TODAY AND HOW
I CAN LEARN OR GROW FROM THIS:

_____
_____
_____

MORNING REFLECTION

DATE ___ / ___ / ___

MY PURPOSE OR INTENTION FOR TODAY:

_____

_____

_____

GOALS ALIGNED WITH MY PURPOSE:

_____   _____

_____   _____

_____   _____

ACTION STEPS I CAN TAKE TODAY:

☐ _____   ☐ _____

☐ _____   ☐ _____

☐ _____   ☐ _____

A SELF-CARE GOAL FOR TODAY:

_____

_____

A CHALLENGE I'M FACING: SOMETHING I'M EXCITED ABOUT:

_____   _____

_____   _____

_____   _____

HOW I SPENT MY TIME TODAY:

☐ MY LIFE'S PASSION   ☐ WORKING   ☐ TIME WITH FRIENDS/FAMILY

☐ VOLUNTEERING   ☐ SELF-CARE   ☐ TIME OUTDOORS

☐ ONLINE/SOCIAL MEDIA   ☐ DOWN TIME   ☐ OTHER: _____

EVENING REFLECTION

HOW I'M FEELING:

_____

_____

_____

THIS BROUGHT ME THE GREATEST JOY TODAY:

_____

_____

SOMETHING I DID TODAY THAT FELT MEANINGFUL:

_____

_____

_____

WHAT I DID TODAY THAT ALIGNED WITH MY PURPOSE:

_____

_____

_____

A NOTABLE RESULT FROM LIVING MY PURPOSE:

_____

_____

_____

A SETBACK I FACED TODAY AND HOW
I CAN LEARN OR GROW FROM THIS:

_____

_____

_____

MORNING REFLECTION

DATE ___ / ___ / ___

MY PURPOSE OR INTENTION FOR TODAY:

_____
_____
_____

GOALS ALIGNED WITH MY PURPOSE:

_____   _____
_____   _____
_____   _____

ACTION STEPS I CAN TAKE TODAY:

☐ _____   ☐ _____
☐ _____   ☐ _____
☐ _____   ☐ _____

A SELF-CARE GOAL FOR TODAY:

_____
_____

A CHALLENGE I'M FACING: SOMETHING I'M EXCITED ABOUT:

_____   _____
_____   _____
_____   _____

HOW I SPENT MY TIME TODAY:

☐ MY LIFE'S PASSION   ☐ WORKING   ☐ TIME WITH FRIENDS/FAMILY
☐ VOLUNTEERING   ☐ SELF-CARE   ☐ TIME OUTDOORS
☐ ONLINE/SOCIAL MEDIA   ☐ DOWN TIME   ☐ OTHER: _____

EVENING REFLECTION

HOW I'M FEELING:

_____
_____
_____

THIS BROUGHT ME THE GREATEST JOY TODAY:

_____
_____

SOMETHING I DID TODAY THAT FELT MEANINGFUL:

_____
_____
_____

WHAT I DID TODAY THAT ALIGNED WITH MY PURPOSE:

_____
_____
_____

A NOTABLE RESULT FROM LIVING MY PURPOSE:

_____
_____
_____

A SETBACK I FACED TODAY AND HOW
I CAN LEARN OR GROW FROM THIS:

_____
_____
_____
_____

MORNING REFLECTION

DATE ___/___/___

MY PURPOSE OR INTENTION FOR TODAY:

_____

_____

_____

GOALS ALIGNED WITH MY PURPOSE:

_____   _____

_____   _____

_____   _____

ACTION STEPS I CAN TAKE TODAY:

☐ _____   ☐ _____
☐ _____   ☐ _____
☐ _____   ☐ _____

A SELF-CARE GOAL FOR TODAY:

_____

_____

A CHALLENGE I'M FACING: SOMETHING I'M EXCITED ABOUT:

_____   _____

_____   _____

_____   _____

HOW I SPENT MY TIME TODAY:

☐ MY LIFE'S PASSION   ☐ WORKING   ☐ TIME WITH FRIENDS/FAMILY
☐ VOLUNTEERING   ☐ SELF-CARE   ☐ TIME OUTDOORS
☐ ONLINE/SOCIAL MEDIA   ☐ DOWN TIME   ☐ OTHER: _____

EVENING REFLECTION

HOW I'M FEELING:

_____
_____
_____

THIS BROUGHT ME THE GREATEST JOY TODAY:

_____
_____

SOMETHING I DID TODAY THAT FELT MEANINGFUL:

_____
_____
_____

WHAT I DID TODAY THAT ALIGNED WITH MY PURPOSE:

_____
_____
_____

A NOTABLE RESULT FROM LIVING MY PURPOSE:

_____
_____
_____

A SETBACK I FACED TODAY AND HOW
I CAN LEARN OR GROW FROM THIS:

_____
_____
_____

MORNING REFLECTION

DATE ___/___/___

MY PURPOSE OR INTENTION FOR TODAY:

_____

_____

_____

GOALS ALIGNED WITH MY PURPOSE:

_____   _____

_____   _____

_____   _____

ACTION STEPS I CAN TAKE TODAY:

☐ _____   ☐ _____

☐ _____   ☐ _____

☐ _____   ☐ _____

A SELF-CARE GOAL FOR TODAY:

_____

_____

A CHALLENGE I'M FACING:

_____

_____

_____

SOMETHING I'M EXCITED ABOUT:

_____

_____

_____

HOW I SPENT MY TIME TODAY:

☐ MY LIFE'S PASSION   ☐ WORKING   ☐ TIME WITH FRIENDS/FAMILY

☐ VOLUNTEERING   ☐ SELF-CARE   ☐ TIME OUTDOORS

☐ ONLINE/SOCIAL MEDIA   ☐ DOWN TIME   ☐ OTHER: _____

EVENING REFLECTION

HOW I'M FEELING:

_____

_____

_____

THIS BROUGHT ME THE GREATEST JOY TODAY:

_____

_____

SOMETHING I DID TODAY THAT FELT MEANINGFUL:

_____

_____

_____

WHAT I DID TODAY THAT ALIGNED WITH MY PURPOSE:

_____

_____

_____

A NOTABLE RESULT FROM LIVING MY PURPOSE:

_____

_____

_____

A SETBACK I FACED TODAY AND HOW
I CAN LEARN OR GROW FROM THIS:

_____

_____

_____

_____

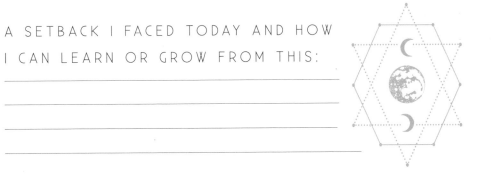

MORNING REFLECTION

DATE ___/___/___

MY PURPOSE OR INTENTION FOR TODAY:

_____

_____

_____

GOALS ALIGNED WITH MY PURPOSE:

_____   _____

_____   _____

_____   _____

ACTION STEPS I CAN TAKE TODAY:

☐ _____   ☐ _____

☐ _____   ☐ _____

☐ _____   ☐ _____

A SELF-CARE GOAL FOR TODAY:

_____

_____

A CHALLENGE I'M FACING: SOMETHING I'M EXCITED ABOUT:

_____   _____

_____   _____

_____   _____

HOW I SPENT MY TIME TODAY:

☐ MY LIFE'S PASSION   ☐ WORKING   ☐ TIME WITH FRIENDS/FAMILY

☐ VOLUNTEERING   ☐ SELF-CARE   ☐ TIME OUTDOORS

☐ ONLINE/SOCIAL MEDIA   ☐ DOWN TIME   ☐ OTHER: _____

EVENING REFLECTION

HOW I'M FEELING:

_____
_____
_____

THIS BROUGHT ME THE GREATEST JOY TODAY:

_____
_____

SOMETHING I DID TODAY THAT FELT MEANINGFUL:

_____
_____
_____

WHAT I DID TODAY THAT ALIGNED WITH MY PURPOSE:

_____
_____
_____

A NOTABLE RESULT FROM LIVING MY PURPOSE:

_____
_____
_____

A SETBACK I FACED TODAY AND HOW
I CAN LEARN OR GROW FROM THIS:

_____
_____
_____

MORNING REFLECTION

DATE ___ / ___ / ___

MY PURPOSE OR INTENTION FOR TODAY:

_____

_____

_____

GOALS ALIGNED WITH MY PURPOSE:

_____   _____

_____   _____

_____   _____

ACTION STEPS I CAN TAKE TODAY:

☐ _____   ☐ _____

☐ _____   ☐ _____

☐ _____   ☐ _____

A SELF-CARE GOAL FOR TODAY:

_____

_____

A CHALLENGE I'M FACING: SOMETHING I'M EXCITED ABOUT:

_____   _____

_____   _____

_____   _____

HOW I SPENT MY TIME TODAY:

☐ MY LIFE'S PASSION   ☐ WORKING   ☐ TIME WITH FRIENDS/FAMILY

☐ VOLUNTEERING   ☐ SELF-CARE   ☐ TIME OUTDOORS

☐ ONLINE/SOCIAL MEDIA   ☐ DOWN TIME   ☐ OTHER: _____

EVENING REFLECTION

HOW I'M FEELING:

_____

_____

_____

THIS BROUGHT ME THE GREATEST JOY TODAY:

_____

_____

SOMETHING I DID TODAY THAT FELT MEANINGFUL:

_____

_____

_____

WHAT I DID TODAY THAT ALIGNED WITH MY PURPOSE:

_____

_____

_____

A NOTABLE RESULT FROM LIVING MY PURPOSE:

_____

_____

_____

A SETBACK I FACED TODAY AND HOW
I CAN LEARN OR GROW FROM THIS:

_____

_____

_____

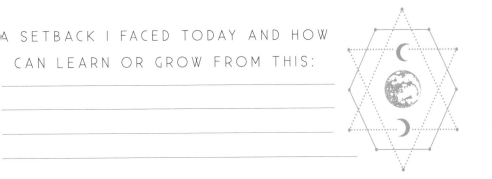

MORNING REFLECTION

DATE ___ / ___ /

MY PURPOSE OR INTENTION FOR TODAY:

_____

_____

_____

GOALS ALIGNED WITH MY PURPOSE:

_____   _____

_____   _____

_____   _____

ACTION STEPS I CAN TAKE TODAY:

☐ _____   ☐ _____

☐ _____   ☐ _____

☐ _____   ☐ _____

A SELF-CARE GOAL FOR TODAY:

_____

_____

A CHALLENGE I'M FACING: SOMETHING I'M EXCITED ABOUT:

_____   _____

_____   _____

_____   _____

HOW I SPENT MY TIME TODAY:

☐ MY LIFE'S PASSION   ☐ WORKING   ☐ TIME WITH FRIENDS/FAMILY

☐ VOLUNTEERING   ☐ SELF-CARE   ☐ TIME OUTDOORS

☐ ONLINE/SOCIAL MEDIA   ☐ DOWN TIME   ☐ OTHER: _____

EVENING REFLECTION

HOW I'M FEELING:

_____

_____

_____

THIS BROUGHT ME THE GREATEST JOY TODAY:

_____

_____

SOMETHING I DID TODAY THAT FELT MEANINGFUL:

_____

_____

_____

WHAT I DID TODAY THAT ALIGNED WITH MY PURPOSE:

_____

_____

_____

A NOTABLE RESULT FROM LIVING MY PURPOSE:

_____

_____

_____

A SETBACK I FACED TODAY AND HOW
I CAN LEARN OR GROW FROM THIS:

_____

_____

_____

_____

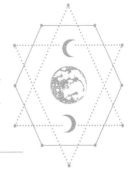

MORNING REFLECTION

DATE ___/___/___

MY PURPOSE OR INTENTION FOR TODAY:

_____

_____

_____

GOALS ALIGNED WITH MY PURPOSE:

_____   _____

_____   _____

_____   _____

ACTION STEPS I CAN TAKE TODAY:

☐ _____   ☐ _____

☐ _____   ☐ _____

☐ _____   ☐ _____

A SELF-CARE GOAL FOR TODAY:

_____

_____

A CHALLENGE I'M FACING: SOMETHING I'M EXCITED ABOUT:

_____   _____

_____   _____

_____   _____

HOW I SPENT MY TIME TODAY:

☐ MY LIFE'S PASSION   ☐ WORKING   ☐ TIME WITH FRIENDS/FAMILY

☐ VOLUNTEERING   ☐ SELF-CARE   ☐ TIME OUTDOORS

☐ ONLINE/SOCIAL MEDIA   ☐ DOWN TIME   ☐ OTHER: _____

EVENING REFLECTION

HOW I'M FEELING:

_____

_____

_____

THIS BROUGHT ME THE GREATEST JOY TODAY:

_____

_____

SOMETHING I DID TODAY THAT FELT MEANINGFUL:

_____

_____

_____

WHAT I DID TODAY THAT ALIGNED WITH MY PURPOSE:

_____

_____

_____

A NOTABLE RESULT FROM LIVING MY PURPOSE:

_____

_____

_____

A SETBACK I FACED TODAY AND HOW
I CAN LEARN OR GROW FROM THIS:

_____

_____

_____

_____

MORNING REFLECTION

DATE ___/___/___

MY PURPOSE OR INTENTION FOR TODAY:

_____
_____
_____

GOALS ALIGNED WITH MY PURPOSE:

_____   _____
_____   _____

ACTION STEPS I CAN TAKE TODAY:

☐ _____   ☐ _____
☐ _____   ☐ _____
☐ _____   ☐ _____

A SELF-CARE GOAL FOR TODAY:

_____
_____

A CHALLENGE I'M FACING:

_____
_____
_____

SOMETHING I'M EXCITED ABOUT:

_____
_____
_____

HOW I SPENT MY TIME TODAY:

☐ MY LIFE'S PASSION   ☐ WORKING   ☐ TIME WITH FRIENDS/FAMILY
☐ VOLUNTEERING   ☐ SELF-CARE   ☐ TIME OUTDOORS
☐ ONLINE/SOCIAL MEDIA   ☐ DOWN TIME   ☐ OTHER:_____

EVENING REFLECTION

HOW I'M FEELING:

_____

_____

_____

THIS BROUGHT ME THE GREATEST JOY TODAY:

_____

_____

SOMETHING I DID TODAY THAT FELT MEANINGFUL:

_____

_____

_____

WHAT I DID TODAY THAT ALIGNED WITH MY PURPOSE:

_____

_____

_____

A NOTABLE RESULT FROM LIVING MY PURPOSE:

_____

_____

_____

A SETBACK I FACED TODAY AND HOW
I CAN LEARN OR GROW FROM THIS:

_____

_____

_____

_____

MORNING REFLECTION

DATE ___/___/___

MY PURPOSE OR INTENTION FOR TODAY:

_____
_____
_____

GOALS ALIGNED WITH MY PURPOSE:

_____   _____
_____   _____
_____   _____

ACTION STEPS I CAN TAKE TODAY:

☐ _____   ☐ _____
☐ _____   ☐ _____
☐ _____   ☐ _____

A SELF-CARE GOAL FOR TODAY:

_____
_____

A CHALLENGE I'M FACING: SOMETHING I'M EXCITED ABOUT:

_____   _____
_____   _____
_____   _____

HOW I SPENT MY TIME TODAY:

☐ MY LIFE'S PASSION   ☐ WORKING   ☐ TIME WITH FRIENDS/FAMILY
☐ VOLUNTEERING   ☐ SELF-CARE   ☐ TIME OUTDOORS
☐ ONLINE/SOCIAL MEDIA   ☐ DOWN TIME   ☐ OTHER: _____

EVENING REFLECTION

HOW I'M FEELING:

_____

_____

_____

THIS BROUGHT ME THE GREATEST JOY TODAY:

_____

_____

SOMETHING I DID TODAY THAT FELT MEANINGFUL:

_____

_____

_____

WHAT I DID TODAY THAT ALIGNED WITH MY PURPOSE:

_____

_____

_____

A NOTABLE RESULT FROM LIVING MY PURPOSE:

_____

_____

_____

A SETBACK I FACED TODAY AND HOW
I CAN LEARN OR GROW FROM THIS:

_____

_____

_____

_____

MORNING REFLECTION

DATE ___/___/___

MY PURPOSE OR INTENTION FOR TODAY:

_____

_____

_____

GOALS ALIGNED WITH MY PURPOSE:

_____ _____

_____ _____

_____ _____

ACTION STEPS I CAN TAKE TODAY:

☐ _____ ☐ _____

☐ _____ ☐ _____

☐ _____ ☐ _____

A SELF-CARE GOAL FOR TODAY:

_____

_____

A CHALLENGE I'M FACING: SOMETHING I'M EXCITED ABOUT:

_____ _____

_____ _____

_____ _____

HOW I SPENT MY TIME TODAY:

☐ MY LIFE'S PASSION   ☐ WORKING   ☐ TIME WITH FRIENDS/FAMILY

☐ VOLUNTEERING   ☐ SELF-CARE   ☐ TIME OUTDOORS

☐ ONLINE/SOCIAL MEDIA   ☐ DOWN TIME   ☐ OTHER: _____

EVENING REFLECTION

HOW I'M FEELING:

_____

_____

_____

THIS BROUGHT ME THE GREATEST JOY TODAY:

_____

_____

SOMETHING I DID TODAY THAT FELT MEANINGFUL:

_____

_____

_____

WHAT I DID TODAY THAT ALIGNED WITH MY PURPOSE:

_____

_____

_____

A NOTABLE RESULT FROM LIVING MY PURPOSE:

_____

_____

_____

A SETBACK I FACED TODAY AND HOW
I CAN LEARN OR GROW FROM THIS:

_____

_____

_____

_____

MORNING REFLECTION

DATE ___/___/___

MY PURPOSE OR INTENTION FOR TODAY:

_____

_____

_____

GOALS ALIGNED WITH MY PURPOSE:

_____   _____

_____   _____

_____   _____

ACTION STEPS I CAN TAKE TODAY:

☐ _____   ☐ _____

☐ _____   ☐ _____

☐ _____   ☐ _____

A SELF-CARE GOAL FOR TODAY:

_____

_____

A CHALLENGE I'M FACING: SOMETHING I'M EXCITED ABOUT:

_____   _____

_____   _____

_____   _____

HOW I SPENT MY TIME TODAY:

☐ MY LIFE'S PASSION   ☐ WORKING   ☐ TIME WITH FRIENDS/FAMILY

☐ VOLUNTEERING   ☐ SELF-CARE   ☐ TIME OUTDOORS

☐ ONLINE/SOCIAL MEDIA   ☐ DOWN TIME   ☐ OTHER: _____

EVENING REFLECTION

HOW I'M FEELING:

_____

_____

_____

THIS BROUGHT ME THE GREATEST JOY TODAY:

_____

_____

SOMETHING I DID TODAY THAT FELT MEANINGFUL:

_____

_____

_____

WHAT I DID TODAY THAT ALIGNED WITH MY PURPOSE:

_____

_____

_____

A NOTABLE RESULT FROM LIVING MY PURPOSE:

_____

_____

_____

A SETBACK I FACED TODAY AND HOW
I CAN LEARN OR GROW FROM THIS:

_____

_____

_____

_____

MORNING REFLECTION

DATE ___/___/___

MY PURPOSE OR INTENTION FOR TODAY:

_____
_____
_____

GOALS ALIGNED WITH MY PURPOSE:

_____   _____
_____   _____
_____   _____

ACTION STEPS I CAN TAKE TODAY:

☐ _____   ☐ _____
☐ _____   ☐ _____
☐ _____   ☐ _____

A SELF-CARE GOAL FOR TODAY:

_____
_____

A CHALLENGE I'M FACING: SOMETHING I'M EXCITED ABOUT:

_____   _____
_____   _____
_____   _____

HOW I SPENT MY TIME TODAY:

☐ MY LIFE'S PASSION   ☐ WORKING   ☐ TIME WITH FRIENDS/FAMILY
☐ VOLUNTEERING   ☐ SELF-CARE   ☐ TIME OUTDOORS
☐ ONLINE/SOCIAL MEDIA   ☐ DOWN TIME   ☐ OTHER: _____

EVENING REFLECTION

HOW I'M FEELING:

_____

_____

_____

THIS BROUGHT ME THE GREATEST JOY TODAY:

_____

_____

SOMETHING I DID TODAY THAT FELT MEANINGFUL:

_____

_____

_____

WHAT I DID TODAY THAT ALIGNED WITH MY PURPOSE:

_____

_____

_____

A NOTABLE RESULT FROM LIVING MY PURPOSE:

_____

_____

_____

A SETBACK I FACED TODAY AND HOW
I CAN LEARN OR GROW FROM THIS:

_____

_____

_____

_____

MORNING REFLECTION

DATE ___/___/___

MY PURPOSE OR INTENTION FOR TODAY:

_____

_____

_____

GOALS ALIGNED WITH MY PURPOSE:

_____   _____

_____   _____

_____   _____

ACTION STEPS I CAN TAKE TODAY:

☐ _____   ☐ _____

☐ _____   ☐ _____

☐ _____   ☐ _____

A SELF-CARE GOAL FOR TODAY:

_____

_____

A CHALLENGE I'M FACING: SOMETHING I'M EXCITED ABOUT:

_____   _____

_____   _____

_____   _____

HOW I SPENT MY TIME TODAY:

☐ MY LIFE'S PASSION   ☐ WORKING   ☐ TIME WITH FRIENDS/FAMILY

☐ VOLUNTEERING   ☐ SELF-CARE   ☐ TIME OUTDOORS

☐ ONLINE/SOCIAL MEDIA   ☐ DOWN TIME   ☐ OTHER:_____

EVENING REFLECTION

HOW I'M FEELING:

_____

_____

_____

THIS BROUGHT ME THE GREATEST JOY TODAY:

_____

_____

SOMETHING I DID TODAY THAT FELT MEANINGFUL:

_____

_____

_____

WHAT I DID TODAY THAT ALIGNED WITH MY PURPOSE:

_____

_____

_____

A NOTABLE RESULT FROM LIVING MY PURPOSE:

_____

_____

_____

A SETBACK I FACED TODAY AND HOW
I CAN LEARN OR GROW FROM THIS:

_____

_____

_____

MORNING REFLECTION

DATE ___/___/___

MY PURPOSE OR INTENTION FOR TODAY:

_____

_____

_____

GOALS ALIGNED WITH MY PURPOSE:

_____   _____

_____   _____

_____   _____

ACTION STEPS I CAN TAKE TODAY:

☐ _____   ☐ _____

☐ _____   ☐ _____

☐ _____   ☐ _____

A SELF-CARE GOAL FOR TODAY:

_____

_____

A CHALLENGE I'M FACING: SOMETHING I'M EXCITED ABOUT:

_____   _____

_____   _____

_____   _____

HOW I SPENT MY TIME TODAY:

☐ MY LIFE'S PASSION   ☐ WORKING   ☐ TIME WITH FRIENDS/FAMILY

☐ VOLUNTEERING   ☐ SELF-CARE   ☐ TIME OUTDOORS

☐ ONLINE/SOCIAL MEDIA   ☐ DOWN TIME   ☐ OTHER: _____

EVENING REFLECTION

HOW I'M FEELING:

_____

_____

_____

THIS BROUGHT ME THE GREATEST JOY TODAY:

_____

_____

SOMETHING I DID TODAY THAT FELT MEANINGFUL:

_____

_____

_____

WHAT I DID TODAY THAT ALIGNED WITH MY PURPOSE:

_____

_____

_____

A NOTABLE RESULT FROM LIVING MY PURPOSE:

_____

_____

_____

A SETBACK I FACED TODAY AND HOW
I CAN LEARN OR GROW FROM THIS:

_____

_____

_____

_____

MORNING REFLECTION

DATE ___/___/___

MY PURPOSE OR INTENTION FOR TODAY:
_____
_____
_____

GOALS ALIGNED WITH MY PURPOSE:
_____   _____
_____   _____
_____   _____

ACTION STEPS I CAN TAKE TODAY:
☐ _____   ☐ _____
☐ _____   ☐ _____
☐ _____   ☐ _____

A SELF-CARE GOAL FOR TODAY:
_____
_____

A CHALLENGE I'M FACING: SOMETHING I'M EXCITED ABOUT:
_____   _____
_____   _____
_____   _____

HOW I SPENT MY TIME TODAY:

☐ MY LIFE'S PASSION   ☐ WORKING   ☐ TIME WITH FRIENDS/FAMILY
☐ VOLUNTEERING   ☐ SELF-CARE   ☐ TIME OUTDOORS
☐ ONLINE/SOCIAL MEDIA   ☐ DOWN TIME   ☐ OTHER:_____

EVENING REFLECTION

HOW I'M FEELING:

_____

_____

_____

THIS BROUGHT ME THE GREATEST JOY TODAY:

_____

_____

SOMETHING I DID TODAY THAT FELT MEANINGFUL:

_____

_____

_____

WHAT I DID TODAY THAT ALIGNED WITH MY PURPOSE:

_____

_____

_____

A NOTABLE RESULT FROM LIVING MY PURPOSE:

_____

_____

_____

A SETBACK I FACED TODAY AND HOW
I CAN LEARN OR GROW FROM THIS:

_____

_____

_____

MORNING REFLECTION

DATE ___/___/___

MY PURPOSE OR INTENTION FOR TODAY:

_____

_____

_____

GOALS ALIGNED WITH MY PURPOSE:

_____ _____

_____ _____

_____ _____

ACTION STEPS I CAN TAKE TODAY:

☐ _____ ☐ _____

☐ _____ ☐ _____

☐ _____ ☐ _____

A SELF-CARE GOAL FOR TODAY:

_____

_____

A CHALLENGE I'M FACING: SOMETHING I'M EXCITED ABOUT:

_____ _____

_____ _____

HOW I SPENT MY TIME TODAY:

☐ MY LIFE'S PASSION ☐ WORKING ☐ TIME WITH FRIENDS/FAMILY

☐ VOLUNTEERING ☐ SELF-CARE ☐ TIME OUTDOORS

☐ ONLINE/SOCIAL MEDIA ☐ DOWN TIME ☐ OTHER: _____

EVENING REFLECTION

HOW I'M FEELING:

_____

_____

_____

THIS BROUGHT ME THE GREATEST JOY TODAY:

_____

_____

SOMETHING I DID TODAY THAT FELT MEANINGFUL:

_____

_____

_____

WHAT I DID TODAY THAT ALIGNED WITH MY PURPOSE:

_____

_____

_____

A NOTABLE RESULT FROM LIVING MY PURPOSE:

_____

_____

_____

A SETBACK I FACED TODAY AND HOW
I CAN LEARN OR GROW FROM THIS:

_____

_____

_____

_____

MORNING REFLECTION

DATE ___/___/___

MY PURPOSE OR INTENTION FOR TODAY:
_____
_____
_____

GOALS ALIGNED WITH MY PURPOSE:
_____   _____
_____   _____
_____   _____

ACTION STEPS I CAN TAKE TODAY:
☐ _____   ☐ _____
☐ _____   ☐ _____
☐ _____   ☐ _____

A SELF-CARE GOAL FOR TODAY:
_____
_____

A CHALLENGE I'M FACING: SOMETHING I'M EXCITED ABOUT:
_____   _____
_____   _____
_____   _____

HOW I SPENT MY TIME TODAY:

☐ MY LIFE'S PASSION   ☐ WORKING   ☐ TIME WITH FRIENDS/FAMILY
☐ VOLUNTEERING   ☐ SELF-CARE   ☐ TIME OUTDOORS
☐ ONLINE/SOCIAL MEDIA   ☐ DOWN TIME   ☐ OTHER: _____

EVENING REFLECTION

HOW I'M FEELING:

_____
_____
_____

THIS BROUGHT ME THE GREATEST JOY TODAY:

_____
_____

SOMETHING I DID TODAY THAT FELT MEANINGFUL:

_____
_____
_____

WHAT I DID TODAY THAT ALIGNED WITH MY PURPOSE:

_____
_____
_____

A NOTABLE RESULT FROM LIVING MY PURPOSE:

_____
_____
_____

A SETBACK I FACED TODAY AND HOW
I CAN LEARN OR GROW FROM THIS:

_____
_____
_____

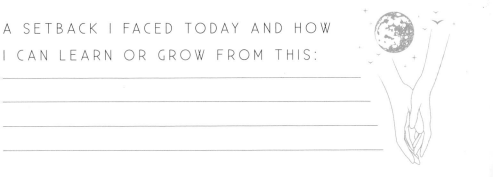

MORNING REFLECTION

DATE ___/___/___

MY PURPOSE OR INTENTION FOR TODAY:
_____
_____
_____

GOALS ALIGNED WITH MY PURPOSE:
_____ _____
_____ _____
_____ _____

ACTION STEPS I CAN TAKE TODAY:
☐ _____ ☐ _____
☐ _____ ☐ _____
☐ _____ ☐ _____

A SELF-CARE GOAL FOR TODAY:
_____
_____

A CHALLENGE I'M FACING: SOMETHING I'M EXCITED ABOUT:
_____ _____
_____ _____
_____ _____

HOW I SPENT MY TIME TODAY:

☐ MY LIFE'S PASSION   ☐ WORKING   ☐ TIME WITH FRIENDS/FAMILY
☐ VOLUNTEERING   ☐ SELF-CARE   ☐ TIME OUTDOORS
☐ ONLINE/SOCIAL MEDIA   ☐ DOWN TIME   ☐ OTHER: _____

EVENING REFLECTION

HOW I'M FEELING:

_____

_____

_____

THIS BROUGHT ME THE GREATEST JOY TODAY:

_____

_____

SOMETHING I DID TODAY THAT FELT MEANINGFUL:

_____

_____

_____

WHAT I DID TODAY THAT ALIGNED WITH MY PURPOSE:

_____

_____

_____

A NOTABLE RESULT FROM LIVING MY PURPOSE:

_____

_____

_____

A SETBACK I FACED TODAY AND HOW
I CAN LEARN OR GROW FROM THIS:

_____

_____

_____

_____

MORNING REFLECTION

DATE ___ / ___ / ___

MY PURPOSE OR INTENTION FOR TODAY:
_____
_____
_____

GOALS ALIGNED WITH MY PURPOSE:
_____   _____
_____   _____
_____   _____

ACTION STEPS I CAN TAKE TODAY:

☐ _____   ☐ _____
☐ _____   ☐ _____
☐ _____   ☐ _____

A SELF-CARE GOAL FOR TODAY:
_____
_____

A CHALLENGE I'M FACING: SOMETHING I'M EXCITED ABOUT:
_____   _____
_____   _____
_____   _____

HOW I SPENT MY TIME TODAY:

☐ MY LIFE'S PASSION   ☐ WORKING   ☐ TIME WITH FRIENDS/FAMILY
☐ VOLUNTEERING   ☐ SELF-CARE   ☐ TIME OUTDOORS
☐ ONLINE/SOCIAL MEDIA   ☐ DOWN TIME   ☐ OTHER: _____

EVENING REFLECTION

HOW I'M FEELING:

_____

_____

_____

THIS BROUGHT ME THE GREATEST JOY TODAY:

_____

_____

SOMETHING I DID TODAY THAT FELT MEANINGFUL:

_____

_____

_____

WHAT I DID TODAY THAT ALIGNED WITH MY PURPOSE:

_____

_____

_____

A NOTABLE RESULT FROM LIVING MY PURPOSE:

_____

_____

_____

A SETBACK I FACED TODAY AND HOW
I CAN LEARN OR GROW FROM THIS:

_____

_____

_____

_____

MORNING REFLECTION

DATE ___/___/___

MY PURPOSE OR INTENTION FOR TODAY:

_____

_____

_____

GOALS ALIGNED WITH MY PURPOSE:

_____   _____

_____   _____

_____   _____

ACTION STEPS I CAN TAKE TODAY:

☐ _____   ☐ _____

☐ _____   ☐ _____

☐ _____   ☐ _____

A SELF-CARE GOAL FOR TODAY:

_____

_____

A CHALLENGE I'M FACING: SOMETHING I'M EXCITED ABOUT:

_____   _____

_____   _____

_____   _____

HOW I SPENT MY TIME TODAY:

☐ MY LIFE'S PASSION   ☐ WORKING   ☐ TIME WITH FRIENDS/FAMILY

☐ VOLUNTEERING   ☐ SELF-CARE   ☐ TIME OUTDOORS

☐ ONLINE/SOCIAL MEDIA   ☐ DOWN TIME   ☐ OTHER: _____

EVENING REFLECTION

HOW I'M FEELING:

_____

_____

_____

THIS BROUGHT ME THE GREATEST JOY TODAY:

_____

_____

SOMETHING I DID TODAY THAT FELT MEANINGFUL:

_____

_____

_____

WHAT I DID TODAY THAT ALIGNED WITH MY PURPOSE:

_____

_____

_____

A NOTABLE RESULT FROM LIVING MY PURPOSE:

_____

_____

_____

A SETBACK I FACED TODAY AND HOW
I CAN LEARN OR GROW FROM THIS:

_____

_____

_____

_____

MORNING REFLECTION

DATE ___ / ___ / ___

MY PURPOSE OR INTENTION FOR TODAY:

_____

_____

_____

GOALS ALIGNED WITH MY PURPOSE:

_____   _____

_____   _____

_____   _____

ACTION STEPS I CAN TAKE TODAY:

☐ _____   ☐ _____

☐ _____   ☐ _____

☐ _____   ☐ _____

A SELF-CARE GOAL FOR TODAY:

_____

_____

A CHALLENGE I'M FACING: SOMETHING I'M EXCITED ABOUT:

_____   _____

_____   _____

_____   _____

HOW I SPENT MY TIME TODAY:

☐ MY LIFE'S PASSION   ☐ WORKING   ☐ TIME WITH FRIENDS/FAMILY

☐ VOLUNTEERING   ☐ SELF-CARE   ☐ TIME OUTDOORS

☐ ONLINE/SOCIAL MEDIA   ☐ DOWN TIME   ☐ OTHER: _____

EVENING REFLECTION

HOW I'M FEELING:

_____
_____
_____

THIS BROUGHT ME THE GREATEST JOY TODAY:

_____
_____

SOMETHING I DID TODAY THAT FELT MEANINGFUL:

_____
_____
_____

WHAT I DID TODAY THAT ALIGNED WITH MY PURPOSE:

_____
_____
_____

A NOTABLE RESULT FROM LIVING MY PURPOSE:

_____
_____
_____

A SETBACK I FACED TODAY AND HOW
I CAN LEARN OR GROW FROM THIS:

_____
_____
_____
_____

MORNING REFLECTION

DATE ___ / ___ /

MY PURPOSE OR INTENTION FOR TODAY:

_____
_____
_____

GOALS ALIGNED WITH MY PURPOSE:

_____   _____
_____   _____
_____   _____

ACTION STEPS I CAN TAKE TODAY:

☐ _____   ☐ _____
☐ _____   ☐ _____
☐ _____   ☐ _____

A SELF-CARE GOAL FOR TODAY:

_____
_____

A CHALLENGE I'M FACING: SOMETHING I'M EXCITED ABOUT:

_____   _____
_____   _____
_____   _____

HOW I SPENT MY TIME TODAY:

☐ MY LIFE'S PASSION   ☐ WORKING   ☐ TIME WITH FRIENDS/FAMILY
☐ VOLUNTEERING   ☐ SELF-CARE   ☐ TIME OUTDOORS
☐ ONLINE/SOCIAL MEDIA   ☐ DOWN TIME   ☐ OTHER: _____

EVENING REFLECTION

HOW I'M FEELING:

_____
_____
_____

THIS BROUGHT ME THE GREATEST JOY TODAY:

_____
_____

SOMETHING I DID TODAY THAT FELT MEANINGFUL:

_____
_____
_____

WHAT I DID TODAY THAT ALIGNED WITH MY PURPOSE:

_____
_____
_____

A NOTABLE RESULT FROM LIVING MY PURPOSE:

_____
_____
_____

A SETBACK I FACED TODAY AND HOW
I CAN LEARN OR GROW FROM THIS:

_____
_____
_____

MORNING REFLECTION

DATE ___ / ___ / ___

MY PURPOSE OR INTENTION FOR TODAY:
_____
_____
_____

GOALS ALIGNED WITH MY PURPOSE:
_____   _____
_____   _____
_____   _____

ACTION STEPS I CAN TAKE TODAY:
☐ _____   ☐ _____
☐ _____   ☐ _____
☐ _____   ☐ _____

A SELF-CARE GOAL FOR TODAY:
_____
_____

A CHALLENGE I'M FACING: SOMETHING I'M EXCITED ABOUT:
_____   _____
_____   _____
_____   _____

HOW I SPENT MY TIME TODAY:

☐ MY LIFE'S PASSION   ☐ WORKING   ☐ TIME WITH FRIENDS/FAMILY
☐ VOLUNTEERING   ☐ SELF-CARE   ☐ TIME OUTDOORS
☐ ONLINE/SOCIAL MEDIA   ☐ DOWN TIME   ☐ OTHER: _____

EVENING REFLECTION

HOW I'M FEELING:

_____

_____

_____

THIS BROUGHT ME THE GREATEST JOY TODAY:

_____

_____

SOMETHING I DID TODAY THAT FELT MEANINGFUL:

_____

_____

_____

WHAT I DID TODAY THAT ALIGNED WITH MY PURPOSE:

_____

_____

_____

A NOTABLE RESULT FROM LIVING MY PURPOSE:

_____

_____

_____

A SETBACK I FACED TODAY AND HOW
I CAN LEARN OR GROW FROM THIS:

_____

_____

_____

MORNING REFLECTION

DATE ___ / ___ / ___

MY PURPOSE OR INTENTION FOR TODAY:

_____

_____

_____

GOALS ALIGNED WITH MY PURPOSE:

_____   _____

_____   _____

_____   _____

ACTION STEPS I CAN TAKE TODAY:

☐ _____   ☐ _____

☐ _____   ☐ _____

☐ _____   ☐ _____

A SELF-CARE GOAL FOR TODAY:

_____

_____

A CHALLENGE I'M FACING: SOMETHING I'M EXCITED ABOUT:

_____   _____

_____   _____

_____   _____

HOW I SPENT MY TIME TODAY:

☐ MY LIFE'S PASSION   ☐ WORKING   ☐ TIME WITH FRIENDS/FAMILY

☐ VOLUNTEERING   ☐ SELF-CARE   ☐ TIME OUTDOORS

☐ ONLINE/SOCIAL MEDIA   ☐ DOWN TIME   ☐ OTHER: _____

EVENING REFLECTION

HOW I'M FEELING:

_____

_____

_____

THIS BROUGHT ME THE GREATEST JOY TODAY:

_____

_____

SOMETHING I DID TODAY THAT FELT MEANINGFUL:

_____

_____

_____

WHAT I DID TODAY THAT ALIGNED WITH MY PURPOSE:

_____

_____

_____

A NOTABLE RESULT FROM LIVING MY PURPOSE:

_____

_____

_____

A SETBACK I FACED TODAY AND HOW
I CAN LEARN OR GROW FROM THIS:

_____

_____

_____

_____

MORNING REFLECTION

DATE ___ / ___ / ___

MY PURPOSE OR INTENTION FOR TODAY:

_____

_____

_____

GOALS ALIGNED WITH MY PURPOSE:

_____ _____

_____ _____

_____ _____

ACTION STEPS I CAN TAKE TODAY:

☐ _____ ☐ _____

☐ _____ ☐ _____

☐ _____ ☐ _____

A SELF-CARE GOAL FOR TODAY:

_____

_____

A CHALLENGE I'M FACING: SOMETHING I'M EXCITED ABOUT:

_____ _____

_____ _____

_____ _____

HOW I SPENT MY TIME TODAY:

☐ MY LIFE'S PASSION   ☐ WORKING   ☐ TIME WITH FRIENDS/FAMILY

☐ VOLUNTEERING   ☐ SELF-CARE   ☐ TIME OUTDOORS

☐ ONLINE/SOCIAL MEDIA   ☐ DOWN TIME   ☐ OTHER: _____

EVENING REFLECTION

HOW I'M FEELING:

_____

_____

_____

THIS BROUGHT ME THE GREATEST JOY TODAY:

_____

_____

SOMETHING I DID TODAY THAT FELT MEANINGFUL:

_____

_____

_____

WHAT I DID TODAY THAT ALIGNED WITH MY PURPOSE:

_____

_____

_____

A NOTABLE RESULT FROM LIVING MY PURPOSE:

_____

_____

_____

A SETBACK I FACED TODAY AND HOW
I CAN LEARN OR GROW FROM THIS:

_____

_____

_____

_____

MORNING REFLECTION

DATE ___ / ___ / ___

MY PURPOSE OR INTENTION FOR TODAY:

_____

_____

_____

GOALS ALIGNED WITH MY PURPOSE:

_____   _____

_____   _____

_____   _____

ACTION STEPS I CAN TAKE TODAY:

☐ _____   ☐ _____

☐ _____   ☐ _____

☐ _____   ☐ _____

A SELF-CARE GOAL FOR TODAY:

_____

_____

A CHALLENGE I'M FACING: SOMETHING I'M EXCITED ABOUT:

_____   _____

_____   _____

_____   _____

HOW I SPENT MY TIME TODAY:

☐ MY LIFE'S PASSION   ☐ WORKING   ☐ TIME WITH FRIENDS/FAMILY

☐ VOLUNTEERING   ☐ SELF-CARE   ☐ TIME OUTDOORS

☐ ONLINE/SOCIAL MEDIA   ☐ DOWN TIME   ☐ OTHER: _____

EVENING REFLECTION

HOW I'M FEELING:

_____

_____

_____

THIS BROUGHT ME THE GREATEST JOY TODAY:

_____

_____

SOMETHING I DID TODAY THAT FELT MEANINGFUL:

_____

_____

_____

WHAT I DID TODAY THAT ALIGNED WITH MY PURPOSE:

_____

_____

_____

A NOTABLE RESULT FROM LIVING MY PURPOSE:

_____

_____

_____

A SETBACK I FACED TODAY AND HOW
I CAN LEARN OR GROW FROM THIS:

_____

_____

_____

MORNING REFLECTION

DATE ___/___/___

MY PURPOSE OR INTENTION FOR TODAY:

_____

_____

_____

GOALS ALIGNED WITH MY PURPOSE:

_____   _____

_____   _____

_____   _____

ACTION STEPS I CAN TAKE TODAY:

☐ _____   ☐ _____

☐ _____   ☐ _____

☐ _____   ☐ _____

A SELF-CARE GOAL FOR TODAY:

_____

_____

A CHALLENGE I'M FACING:

_____

_____

_____

SOMETHING I'M EXCITED ABOUT:

_____

_____

_____

HOW I SPENT MY TIME TODAY:

☐ MY LIFE'S PASSION   ☐ WORKING   ☐ TIME WITH FRIENDS/FAMILY

☐ VOLUNTEERING   ☐ SELF-CARE   ☐ TIME OUTDOORS

☐ ONLINE/SOCIAL MEDIA   ☐ DOWN TIME   ☐ OTHER: _____

EVENING REFLECTION

HOW I'M FEELING:

_____
_____
_____

THIS BROUGHT ME THE GREATEST JOY TODAY:

_____
_____

SOMETHING I DID TODAY THAT FELT MEANINGFUL:

_____
_____
_____

WHAT I DID TODAY THAT ALIGNED WITH MY PURPOSE:

_____
_____
_____

A NOTABLE RESULT FROM LIVING MY PURPOSE:

_____
_____
_____

A SETBACK I FACED TODAY AND HOW
I CAN LEARN OR GROW FROM THIS:

_____
_____
_____
_____

MORNING REFLECTION

DATE ___ / ___ /___

MY PURPOSE OR INTENTION FOR TODAY:

_____

_____

_____

GOALS ALIGNED WITH MY PURPOSE:

_____   _____

_____   _____

_____   _____

ACTION STEPS I CAN TAKE TODAY:

☐ _____   ☐ _____

☐ _____   ☐ _____

☐ _____   ☐ _____

A SELF-CARE GOAL FOR TODAY:

_____

_____

A CHALLENGE I'M FACING: SOMETHING I'M EXCITED ABOUT:

_____   _____

_____   _____

_____   _____

HOW I SPENT MY TIME TODAY:

☐ MY LIFE'S PASSION   ☐ WORKING   ☐ TIME WITH FRIENDS/FAMILY

☐ VOLUNTEERING   ☐ SELF-CARE   ☐ TIME OUTDOORS

☐ ONLINE/SOCIAL MEDIA   ☐ DOWN TIME   ☐ OTHER: _____

EVENING REFLECTION

HOW I'M FEELING:

_____
_____
_____

THIS BROUGHT ME THE GREATEST JOY TODAY:

_____
_____

SOMETHING I DID TODAY THAT FELT MEANINGFUL:

_____
_____
_____

WHAT I DID TODAY THAT ALIGNED WITH MY PURPOSE:

_____
_____
_____

A NOTABLE RESULT FROM LIVING MY PURPOSE:

_____
_____
_____

A SETBACK I FACED TODAY AND HOW
I CAN LEARN OR GROW FROM THIS:

_____
_____
_____

MORNING REFLECTION

DATE ___/___/___

MY PURPOSE OR INTENTION FOR TODAY:

_____

_____

_____

GOALS ALIGNED WITH MY PURPOSE:

_____   _____

_____   _____

_____   _____

ACTION STEPS I CAN TAKE TODAY:

☐ _____   ☐ _____

☐ _____   ☐ _____

☐ _____   ☐ _____

A SELF-CARE GOAL FOR TODAY:

_____

_____

A CHALLENGE I'M FACING: SOMETHING I'M EXCITED ABOUT:

_____   _____

_____   _____

_____   _____

HOW I SPENT MY TIME TODAY:

☐ MY LIFE'S PASSION   ☐ WORKING   ☐ TIME WITH FRIENDS/FAMILY

☐ VOLUNTEERING   ☐ SELF-CARE   ☐ TIME OUTDOORS

☐ ONLINE/SOCIAL MEDIA   ☐ DOWN TIME   ☐ OTHER: _____

EVENING REFLECTION

HOW I'M FEELING:

_____

_____

_____

THIS BROUGHT ME THE GREATEST JOY TODAY:

_____

_____

SOMETHING I DID TODAY THAT FELT MEANINGFUL:

_____

_____

_____

WHAT I DID TODAY THAT ALIGNED WITH MY PURPOSE:

_____

_____

_____

A NOTABLE RESULT FROM LIVING MY PURPOSE:

_____

_____

_____

A SETBACK I FACED TODAY AND HOW
I CAN LEARN OR GROW FROM THIS:

_____

_____

_____

MORNING REFLECTION

DATE ___ / ___ /___

MY PURPOSE OR INTENTION FOR TODAY:

_____

_____

_____

GOALS ALIGNED WITH MY PURPOSE:

_____   _____

_____   _____

_____   _____

ACTION STEPS I CAN TAKE TODAY:

☐ _____   ☐ _____

☐ _____   ☐ _____

☐ _____   ☐ _____

A SELF-CARE GOAL FOR TODAY:

_____

_____

A CHALLENGE I'M FACING: SOMETHING I'M EXCITED ABOUT:

_____   _____

_____   _____

_____   _____

HOW I SPENT MY TIME TODAY:

☐ MY LIFE'S PASSION   ☐ WORKING   ☐ TIME WITH FRIENDS/FAMILY

☐ VOLUNTEERING   ☐ SELF-CARE   ☐ TIME OUTDOORS

☐ ONLINE/SOCIAL MEDIA ☐ DOWN TIME   ☐ OTHER: _____

EVENING REFLECTION

HOW I'M FEELING:

_____
_____
_____

THIS BROUGHT ME THE GREATEST JOY TODAY:

_____
_____

SOMETHING I DID TODAY THAT FELT MEANINGFUL:

_____
_____
_____

WHAT I DID TODAY THAT ALIGNED WITH MY PURPOSE:

_____
_____
_____

A NOTABLE RESULT FROM LIVING MY PURPOSE:

_____
_____
_____

A SETBACK I FACED TODAY AND HOW
I CAN LEARN OR GROW FROM THIS:

_____
_____
_____

MORNING REFLECTION

DATE ___/___/___

MY PURPOSE OR INTENTION FOR TODAY:

_____

_____

_____

GOALS ALIGNED WITH MY PURPOSE:

_____   _____

_____   _____

_____   _____

ACTION STEPS I CAN TAKE TODAY:

☐ _____   ☐ _____

☐ _____   ☐ _____

☐ _____   ☐ _____

A SELF-CARE GOAL FOR TODAY:

_____

_____

A CHALLENGE I'M FACING: SOMETHING I'M EXCITED ABOUT:

_____   _____

_____   _____

_____   _____

HOW I SPENT MY TIME TODAY:

☐ MY LIFE'S PASSION   ☐ WORKING   ☐ TIME WITH FRIENDS/FAMILY

☐ VOLUNTEERING   ☐ SELF-CARE   ☐ TIME OUTDOORS

☐ ONLINE/SOCIAL MEDIA   ☐ DOWN TIME   ☐ OTHER: _____

EVENING REFLECTION

HOW I'M FEELING:

_____

_____

_____

THIS BROUGHT ME THE GREATEST JOY TODAY:

_____

_____

SOMETHING I DID TODAY THAT FELT MEANINGFUL:

_____

_____

_____

WHAT I DID TODAY THAT ALIGNED WITH MY PURPOSE:

_____

_____

_____

A NOTABLE RESULT FROM LIVING MY PURPOSE:

_____

_____

_____

A SETBACK I FACED TODAY AND HOW
I CAN LEARN OR GROW FROM THIS:

_____

_____

_____

_____

MORNING REFLECTION

DATE ___/___/___

MY PURPOSE OR INTENTION FOR TODAY:

_____
_____
_____

GOALS ALIGNED WITH MY PURPOSE:

_____   _____
_____   _____
_____   _____

ACTION STEPS I CAN TAKE TODAY:

☐ _____   ☐ _____
☐ _____   ☐ _____
☐ _____   ☐ _____

A SELF-CARE GOAL FOR TODAY:

_____
_____

A CHALLENGE I'M FACING:

_____
_____
_____

SOMETHING I'M EXCITED ABOUT:

_____
_____
_____

HOW I SPENT MY TIME TODAY:

☐ MY LIFE'S PASSION   ☐ WORKING   ☐ TIME WITH FRIENDS/FAMILY
☐ VOLUNTEERING   ☐ SELF-CARE   ☐ TIME OUTDOORS
☐ ONLINE/SOCIAL MEDIA   ☐ DOWN TIME   ☐ OTHER: _____

EVENING REFLECTION

HOW I'M FEELING:

_____

_____

_____

THIS BROUGHT ME THE GREATEST JOY TODAY:

_____

_____

SOMETHING I DID TODAY THAT FELT MEANINGFUL:

_____

_____

_____

WHAT I DID TODAY THAT ALIGNED WITH MY PURPOSE:

_____

_____

_____

A NOTABLE RESULT FROM LIVING MY PURPOSE:

_____

_____

_____

A SETBACK I FACED TODAY AND HOW
I CAN LEARN OR GROW FROM THIS:

_____

_____

_____

MORNING REFLECTION

DATE ___/___/___

MY PURPOSE OR INTENTION FOR TODAY:

_____

_____

_____

GOALS ALIGNED WITH MY PURPOSE:

_____   _____

_____   _____

_____   _____

ACTION STEPS I CAN TAKE TODAY:

☐ _____   ☐ _____

☐ _____   ☐ _____

☐ _____   ☐ _____

A SELF-CARE GOAL FOR TODAY:

_____

_____

A CHALLENGE I'M FACING: SOMETHING I'M EXCITED ABOUT:

_____   _____

_____   _____

_____   _____

HOW I SPENT MY TIME TODAY:

☐ MY LIFE'S PASSION   ☐ WORKING   ☐ TIME WITH FRIENDS/FAMILY

☐ VOLUNTEERING   ☐ SELF-CARE   ☐ TIME OUTDOORS

☐ ONLINE/SOCIAL MEDIA   ☐ DOWN TIME   ☐ OTHER: _____

EVENING REFLECTION

HOW I'M FEELING:

_____

_____

_____

THIS BROUGHT ME THE GREATEST JOY TODAY:

_____

_____

SOMETHING I DID TODAY THAT FELT MEANINGFUL:

_____

_____

_____

WHAT I DID TODAY THAT ALIGNED WITH MY PURPOSE:

_____

_____

_____

A NOTABLE RESULT FROM LIVING MY PURPOSE:

_____

_____

_____

A SETBACK I FACED TODAY AND HOW
I CAN LEARN OR GROW FROM THIS:

_____

_____

_____

MORNING REFLECTION

DATE ___ / ___ / ___

MY PURPOSE OR INTENTION FOR TODAY:

_____

_____

_____

GOALS ALIGNED WITH MY PURPOSE:

_____   _____

_____   _____

_____   _____

ACTION STEPS I CAN TAKE TODAY:

☐ _____   ☐ _____

☐ _____   ☐ _____

☐ _____   ☐ _____

A SELF-CARE GOAL FOR TODAY:

_____

_____

A CHALLENGE I'M FACING: SOMETHING I'M EXCITED ABOUT:

_____   _____

_____   _____

_____   _____

HOW I SPENT MY TIME TODAY:

☐ MY LIFE'S PASSION   ☐ WORKING   ☐ TIME WITH FRIENDS/FAMILY

☐ VOLUNTEERING   ☐ SELF-CARE   ☐ TIME OUTDOORS

☐ ONLINE/SOCIAL MEDIA   ☐ DOWN TIME   ☐ OTHER: _____

EVENING REFLECTION

HOW I'M FEELING:

_____

_____

THIS BROUGHT ME THE GREATEST JOY TODAY:

_____

_____

SOMETHING I DID TODAY THAT FELT MEANINGFUL:

_____

_____

_____

WHAT I DID TODAY THAT ALIGNED WITH MY PURPOSE:

_____

_____

_____

A NOTABLE RESULT FROM LIVING MY PURPOSE:

_____

_____

_____

A SETBACK I FACED TODAY AND HOW
I CAN LEARN OR GROW FROM THIS:

_____

_____

_____

MORNING REFLECTION

DATE ___ / ___ /___

MY PURPOSE OR INTENTION FOR TODAY:

_____

_____

_____

GOALS ALIGNED WITH MY PURPOSE:

_____   _____

_____   _____

_____   _____

ACTION STEPS I CAN TAKE TODAY:

☐ _____   ☐ _____

☐ _____   ☐ _____

☐ _____   ☐ _____

A SELF-CARE GOAL FOR TODAY:

_____

_____

A CHALLENGE I'M FACING: SOMETHING I'M EXCITED ABOUT:

_____   _____

_____   _____

_____   _____

HOW I SPENT MY TIME TODAY:

☐ MY LIFE'S PASSION   ☐ WORKING   ☐ TIME WITH FRIENDS/FAMILY
☐ VOLUNTEERING   ☐ SELF-CARE   ☐ TIME OUTDOORS
☐ ONLINE/SOCIAL MEDIA   ☐ DOWN TIME   ☐ OTHER: _____

EVENING REFLECTION

HOW I'M FEELING:

_____

_____

_____

THIS BROUGHT ME THE GREATEST JOY TODAY:

_____

_____

SOMETHING I DID TODAY THAT FELT MEANINGFUL:

_____

_____

_____

WHAT I DID TODAY THAT ALIGNED WITH MY PURPOSE:

_____

_____

_____

A NOTABLE RESULT FROM LIVING MY PURPOSE:

_____

_____

_____

A SETBACK I FACED TODAY AND HOW
I CAN LEARN OR GROW FROM THIS:

_____

_____

_____

MORNING REFLECTION

DATE ___/___/___

MY PURPOSE OR INTENTION FOR TODAY:

_____

_____

_____

GOALS ALIGNED WITH MY PURPOSE:

_____   _____

_____   _____

_____   _____

ACTION STEPS I CAN TAKE TODAY:

☐ _____   ☐ _____

☐ _____   ☐ _____

☐ _____   ☐ _____

A SELF-CARE GOAL FOR TODAY:

_____

_____

A CHALLENGE I'M FACING: SOMETHING I'M EXCITED ABOUT:

_____   _____

_____   _____

_____   _____

HOW I SPENT MY TIME TODAY:

☐ MY LIFE'S PASSION   ☐ WORKING   ☐ TIME WITH FRIENDS/FAMILY

☐ VOLUNTEERING   ☐ SELF-CARE   ☐ TIME OUTDOORS

☐ ONLINE/SOCIAL MEDIA   ☐ DOWN TIME   ☐ OTHER: _____

EVENING REFLECTION

HOW I'M FEELING:

_____
_____
_____

THIS BROUGHT ME THE GREATEST JOY TODAY:

_____
_____

SOMETHING I DID TODAY THAT FELT MEANINGFUL:

_____
_____
_____

WHAT I DID TODAY THAT ALIGNED WITH MY PURPOSE:

_____
_____
_____

A NOTABLE RESULT FROM LIVING MY PURPOSE:

_____
_____
_____

A SETBACK I FACED TODAY AND HOW
I CAN LEARN OR GROW FROM THIS:

_____
_____
_____

MORNING REFLECTION

DATE ___ / ___ / ___

MY PURPOSE OR INTENTION FOR TODAY:

_____

_____

_____

GOALS ALIGNED WITH MY PURPOSE:

_____   _____

_____   _____

_____   _____

ACTION STEPS I CAN TAKE TODAY:

☐ _____   ☐ _____

☐ _____   ☐ _____

☐ _____   ☐ _____

A SELF-CARE GOAL FOR TODAY:

_____

_____

A CHALLENGE I'M FACING: SOMETHING I'M EXCITED ABOUT:

_____   _____

_____   _____

_____   _____

HOW I SPENT MY TIME TODAY:

☐ MY LIFE'S PASSION   ☐ WORKING   ☐ TIME WITH FRIENDS/FAMILY

☐ VOLUNTEERING   ☐ SELF-CARE   ☐ TIME OUTDOORS

☐ ONLINE/SOCIAL MEDIA   ☐ DOWN TIME   ☐ OTHER: _____

EVENING REFLECTION

HOW I'M FEELING:

_____

_____

_____

THIS BROUGHT ME THE GREATEST JOY TODAY:

_____

_____

SOMETHING I DID TODAY THAT FELT MEANINGFUL:

_____

_____

_____

WHAT I DID TODAY THAT ALIGNED WITH MY PURPOSE:

_____

_____

_____

A NOTABLE RESULT FROM LIVING MY PURPOSE:

_____

_____

_____

A SETBACK I FACED TODAY AND HOW
I CAN LEARN OR GROW FROM THIS:

_____

_____

_____

_____

MORNING REFLECTION

DATE ___/___/___

MY PURPOSE OR INTENTION FOR TODAY:

_____

_____

_____

GOALS ALIGNED WITH MY PURPOSE:

_____   _____

_____   _____

_____   _____

ACTION STEPS I CAN TAKE TODAY:

☐ _____   ☐ _____

☐ _____   ☐ _____

☐ _____   ☐ _____

A SELF-CARE GOAL FOR TODAY:

_____

_____

A CHALLENGE I'M FACING: SOMETHING I'M EXCITED ABOUT:

_____   _____

_____   _____

HOW I SPENT MY TIME TODAY:

☐ MY LIFE'S PASSION   ☐ WORKING   ☐ TIME WITH FRIENDS/FAMILY

☐ VOLUNTEERING   ☐ SELF-CARE   ☐ TIME OUTDOORS

☐ ONLINE/SOCIAL MEDIA   ☐ DOWN TIME   ☐ OTHER: _____

EVENING REFLECTION

HOW I'M FEELING:

_____

_____

_____

THIS BROUGHT ME THE GREATEST JOY TODAY:

_____

_____

SOMETHING I DID TODAY THAT FELT MEANINGFUL:

_____

_____

_____

WHAT I DID TODAY THAT ALIGNED WITH MY PURPOSE:

_____

_____

_____

A NOTABLE RESULT FROM LIVING MY PURPOSE:

_____

_____

_____

A SETBACK I FACED TODAY AND HOW
I CAN LEARN OR GROW FROM THIS:

_____

_____

_____

MORNING REFLECTION

DATE ___ / ___ / ___

MY PURPOSE OR INTENTION FOR TODAY:

_____

_____

_____

GOALS ALIGNED WITH MY PURPOSE:

_____   _____

_____   _____

_____   _____

ACTION STEPS I CAN TAKE TODAY:

☐ _____   ☐ _____

☐ _____   ☐ _____

☐ _____   ☐ _____

A SELF-CARE GOAL FOR TODAY:

_____

_____

A CHALLENGE I'M FACING: SOMETHING I'M EXCITED ABOUT:

_____   _____

_____   _____

_____   _____

HOW I SPENT MY TIME TODAY:

☐ MY LIFE'S PASSION   ☐ WORKING   ☐ TIME WITH FRIENDS/FAMILY

☐ VOLUNTEERING   ☐ SELF-CARE   ☐ TIME OUTDOORS

☐ ONLINE/SOCIAL MEDIA   ☐ DOWN TIME   ☐ OTHER: _____

EVENING REFLECTION

HOW I'M FEELING:

_____
_____
_____

THIS BROUGHT ME THE GREATEST JOY TODAY:

_____
_____

SOMETHING I DID TODAY THAT FELT MEANINGFUL:

_____
_____
_____

WHAT I DID TODAY THAT ALIGNED WITH MY PURPOSE:

_____
_____
_____

A NOTABLE RESULT FROM LIVING MY PURPOSE:

_____
_____
_____

A SETBACK I FACED TODAY AND HOW
I CAN LEARN OR GROW FROM THIS:

_____
_____
_____

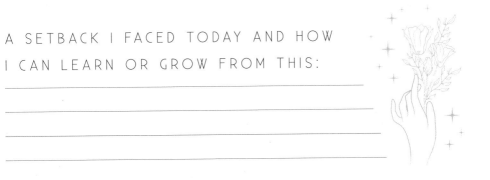

MORNING REFLECTION

DATE ___ / ___ / _

MY PURPOSE OR INTENTION FOR TODAY:

_____

_____

_____

GOALS ALIGNED WITH MY PURPOSE:

_____ _____

_____ _____

_____ _____

ACTION STEPS I CAN TAKE TODAY:

☐ _____ ☐ _____

☐ _____ ☐ _____

☐ _____ ☐ _____

A SELF-CARE GOAL FOR TODAY:

_____

_____

A CHALLENGE I'M FACING: SOMETHING I'M EXCITED ABOUT:

_____ _____

_____ _____

_____ _____

HOW I SPENT MY TIME TODAY:

☐ MY LIFE'S PASSION   ☐ WORKING   ☐ TIME WITH FRIENDS/FAMILY

☐ VOLUNTEERING   ☐ SELF-CARE   ☐ TIME OUTDOORS

☐ ONLINE/SOCIAL MEDIA   ☐ DOWN TIME   ☐ OTHER: _____

EVENING REFLECTION

HOW I'M FEELING:

_____

_____

_____

THIS BROUGHT ME THE GREATEST JOY TODAY:

_____

_____

SOMETHING I DID TODAY THAT FELT MEANINGFUL:

_____

_____

_____

WHAT I DID TODAY THAT ALIGNED WITH MY PURPOSE:

_____

_____

_____

A NOTABLE RESULT FROM LIVING MY PURPOSE:

_____

_____

_____

A SETBACK I FACED TODAY AND HOW
I CAN LEARN OR GROW FROM THIS:

_____

_____

_____

_____

MORNING REFLECTION

DATE ___ / ___ / ___

MY PURPOSE OR INTENTION FOR TODAY:

_____

_____

_____

GOALS ALIGNED WITH MY PURPOSE:

_____   _____

_____   _____

_____   _____

ACTION STEPS I CAN TAKE TODAY:

☐ _____   ☐ _____

☐ _____   ☐ _____

☐ _____   ☐ _____

A SELF-CARE GOAL FOR TODAY:

_____

_____

A CHALLENGE I'M FACING: SOMETHING I'M EXCITED ABOUT:

_____   _____

_____   _____

_____   _____

HOW I SPENT MY TIME TODAY:

☐ MY LIFE'S PASSION   ☐ WORKING   ☐ TIME WITH FRIENDS/FAMILY

☐ VOLUNTEERING   ☐ SELF-CARE   ☐ TIME OUTDOORS

☐ ONLINE/SOCIAL MEDIA   ☐ DOWN TIME   ☐ OTHER: _____

EVENING REFLECTION

HOW I'M FEELING:

_____

_____

_____

THIS BROUGHT ME THE GREATEST JOY TODAY:

_____

_____

SOMETHING I DID TODAY THAT FELT MEANINGFUL:

_____

_____

_____

WHAT I DID TODAY THAT ALIGNED WITH MY PURPOSE:

_____

_____

_____

A NOTABLE RESULT FROM LIVING MY PURPOSE:

_____

_____

_____

A SETBACK I FACED TODAY AND HOW
I CAN LEARN OR GROW FROM THIS:

_____

_____

_____

_____

MORNING REFLECTION

DATE ___ / ___ / ___

MY PURPOSE OR INTENTION FOR TODAY:

_____

_____

_____

GOALS ALIGNED WITH MY PURPOSE:

_____   _____

_____   _____

_____   _____

ACTION STEPS I CAN TAKE TODAY:

☐ _____   ☐ _____

☐ _____   ☐ _____

☐ _____   ☐ _____

A SELF-CARE GOAL FOR TODAY:

_____

_____

A CHALLENGE I'M FACING: SOMETHING I'M EXCITED ABOUT:

_____   _____

_____   _____

_____   _____

HOW I SPENT MY TIME TODAY:

☐ MY LIFE'S PASSION   ☐ WORKING   ☐ TIME WITH FRIENDS/FAMILY

☐ VOLUNTEERING   ☐ SELF-CARE   ☐ TIME OUTDOORS

☐ ONLINE/SOCIAL MEDIA   ☐ DOWN TIME   ☐ OTHER: _____

EVENING REFLECTION

HOW I'M FEELING:

_____
_____
_____

THIS BROUGHT ME THE GREATEST JOY TODAY:

_____
_____

SOMETHING I DID TODAY THAT FELT MEANINGFUL:

_____
_____
_____

WHAT I DID TODAY THAT ALIGNED WITH MY PURPOSE:

_____
_____
_____

A NOTABLE RESULT FROM LIVING MY PURPOSE:

_____
_____

A SETBACK I FACED TODAY AND HOW
I CAN LEARN OR GROW FROM THIS:

_____
_____
_____

MORNING REFLECTION

DATE ___/___/___

MY PURPOSE OR INTENTION FOR TODAY:
_____
_____
_____

GOALS ALIGNED WITH MY PURPOSE:
_____   _____
_____   _____
_____   _____

ACTION STEPS I CAN TAKE TODAY:
☐ _____   ☐ _____
☐ _____   ☐ _____
☐ _____   ☐ _____

A SELF-CARE GOAL FOR TODAY:
_____
_____

A CHALLENGE I'M FACING: SOMETHING I'M EXCITED ABOUT:
_____   _____
_____   _____
_____   _____

HOW I SPENT MY TIME TODAY:

☐ MY LIFE'S PASSION   ☐ WORKING   ☐ TIME WITH FRIENDS/FAMILY
☐ VOLUNTEERING   ☐ SELF-CARE   ☐ TIME OUTDOORS
☐ ONLINE/SOCIAL MEDIA   ☐ DOWN TIME   ☐ OTHER: _____

EVENING REFLECTION

HOW I'M FEELING:

_____
_____
_____

THIS BROUGHT ME THE GREATEST JOY TODAY:

_____
_____

SOMETHING I DID TODAY THAT FELT MEANINGFUL:

_____
_____
_____
_____

WHAT I DID TODAY THAT ALIGNED WITH MY PURPOSE:

_____
_____
_____

A NOTABLE RESULT FROM LIVING MY PURPOSE:

_____
_____
_____

A SETBACK I FACED TODAY AND HOW
I CAN LEARN OR GROW FROM THIS:

_____
_____
_____

MORNING REFLECTION

DATE ___/___/___

MY PURPOSE OR INTENTION FOR TODAY:

_____

_____

_____

GOALS ALIGNED WITH MY PURPOSE:

_____   _____

_____   _____

_____   _____

ACTION STEPS I CAN TAKE TODAY:

☐ _____   ☐ _____

☐ _____   ☐ _____

☐ _____   ☐ _____

A SELF-CARE GOAL FOR TODAY:

_____

_____

A CHALLENGE I'M FACING: SOMETHING I'M EXCITED ABOUT:

_____   _____

_____   _____

_____   _____

HOW I SPENT MY TIME TODAY:

☐ MY LIFE'S PASSION   ☐ WORKING   ☐ TIME WITH FRIENDS/FAMILY

☐ VOLUNTEERING   ☐ SELF-CARE   ☐ TIME OUTDOORS

☐ ONLINE/SOCIAL MEDIA   ☐ DOWN TIME   ☐ OTHER: _____

EVENING REFLECTION

HOW I'M FEELING:

_____
_____
_____

THIS BROUGHT ME THE GREATEST JOY TODAY:

_____
_____

SOMETHING I DID TODAY THAT FELT MEANINGFUL:

_____
_____
_____

WHAT I DID TODAY THAT ALIGNED WITH MY PURPOSE:

_____
_____
_____

A NOTABLE RESULT FROM LIVING MY PURPOSE:

_____
_____
_____

A SETBACK I FACED TODAY AND HOW
I CAN LEARN OR GROW FROM THIS:

_____
_____
_____

MORNING·REFLECTION

DATE ___/___/___

MY PURPOSE OR INTENTION FOR TODAY:

_____

_____

_____

GOALS ALIGNED WITH MY PURPOSE:

_____   _____

_____   _____

_____   _____

ACTION STEPS I CAN TAKE TODAY:

☐ _____   ☐ _____

☐ _____   ☐ _____

☐ _____   ☐ _____

A SELF-CARE GOAL FOR TODAY:

_____

_____

A CHALLENGE I'M FACING: SOMETHING I'M EXCITED ABOUT:

_____   _____

_____   _____

_____   _____

HOW I SPENT MY TIME TODAY:

☐ MY LIFE'S PASSION   ☐ WORKING   ☐ TIME WITH FRIENDS/FAMILY

☐ VOLUNTEERING   ☐ SELF-CARE   ☐ TIME OUTDOORS

☐ ONLINE/SOCIAL MEDIA   ☐ DOWN TIME   ☐ OTHER: _____

EVENING REFLECTION

HOW I'M FEELING:

_____

_____

_____

THIS BROUGHT ME THE GREATEST JOY TODAY:

_____

_____

SOMETHING I DID TODAY THAT FELT MEANINGFUL:

_____

_____

_____

WHAT I DID TODAY THAT ALIGNED WITH MY PURPOSE:

_____

_____

_____

A NOTABLE RESULT FROM LIVING MY PURPOSE:

_____

_____

_____

A SETBACK I FACED TODAY AND HOW
I CAN LEARN OR GROW FROM THIS:

_____

_____

_____

MORNING REFLECTION

DATE ___ / ___ / ___

MY PURPOSE OR INTENTION FOR TODAY:

_____

_____

_____

GOALS ALIGNED WITH MY PURPOSE:

_____   _____

_____   _____

_____   _____

ACTION STEPS I CAN TAKE TODAY:

☐ _____   ☐ _____

☐ _____   ☐ _____

☐ _____   ☐ _____

A SELF-CARE GOAL FOR TODAY:

_____

_____

A CHALLENGE I'M FACING: SOMETHING I'M EXCITED ABOUT:

_____   _____

_____   _____

_____   _____

HOW I SPENT MY TIME TODAY:

☐ MY LIFE'S PASSION   ☐ WORKING   ☐ TIME WITH FRIENDS/FAMILY

☐ VOLUNTEERING   ☐ SELF-CARE   ☐ TIME OUTDOORS

☐ ONLINE/SOCIAL MEDIA   ☐ DOWN TIME   ☐ OTHER: _____

EVENING REFLECTION

HOW I'M FEELING:

_____

_____

_____

THIS BROUGHT ME THE GREATEST JOY TODAY:

_____

_____

SOMETHING I DID TODAY THAT FELT MEANINGFUL:

_____

_____

_____

WHAT I DID TODAY THAT ALIGNED WITH MY PURPOSE:

_____

_____

_____

A NOTABLE RESULT FROM LIVING MY PURPOSE:

_____

_____

_____

A SETBACK I FACED TODAY AND HOW
I CAN LEARN OR GROW FROM THIS:

_____

_____

_____

_____

MORNING REFLECTION

DATE ___/___/___

MY PURPOSE OR INTENTION FOR TODAY:

_____

_____

_____

GOALS ALIGNED WITH MY PURPOSE:

_____   _____

_____   _____

_____   _____

ACTION STEPS I CAN TAKE TODAY:

☐ _____   ☐ _____

☐ _____   ☐ _____

☐ _____   ☐ _____

A SELF-CARE GOAL FOR TODAY:

_____

_____

A CHALLENGE I'M FACING: SOMETHING I'M EXCITED ABOUT:

_____   _____

_____   _____

_____   _____

HOW I SPENT MY TIME TODAY:

☐ MY LIFE'S PASSION   ☐ WORKING   ☐ TIME WITH FRIENDS/FAMILY

☐ VOLUNTEERING   ☐ SELF-CARE   ☐ TIME OUTDOORS

☐ ONLINE/SOCIAL MEDIA   ☐ DOWN TIME   ☐ OTHER: _____

EVENING REFLECTION

HOW I'M FEELING:

_____

_____

_____

THIS BROUGHT ME THE GREATEST JOY TODAY:

_____

_____

SOMETHING I DID TODAY THAT FELT MEANINGFUL:

_____

_____

_____

WHAT I DID TODAY THAT ALIGNED WITH MY PURPOSE:

_____

_____

_____

A NOTABLE RESULT FROM LIVING MY PURPOSE:

_____

_____

_____

A SETBACK I FACED TODAY AND HOW
I CAN LEARN OR GROW FROM THIS:

_____

_____

_____

_____

MORNING REFLECTION

DATE ___ / ___ / ___

MY PURPOSE OR INTENTION FOR TODAY:

_____

_____

_____

GOALS ALIGNED WITH MY PURPOSE:

_____   _____

_____   _____

_____   _____

ACTION STEPS I CAN TAKE TODAY:

☐ _____   ☐ _____

☐ _____   ☐ _____

☐ _____   ☐ _____

A SELF-CARE GOAL FOR TODAY:

_____

_____

A CHALLENGE I'M FACING: SOMETHING I'M EXCITED ABOUT:

_____   _____

_____   _____

_____   _____

HOW I SPENT MY TIME TODAY:

☐ MY LIFE'S PASSION   ☐ WORKING   ☐ TIME WITH FRIENDS/FAMILY

☐ VOLUNTEERING   ☐ SELF-CARE   ☐ TIME OUTDOORS

☐ ONLINE/SOCIAL MEDIA   ☐ DOWN TIME   ☐ OTHER: _____

EVENING REFLECTION

HOW I'M FEELING:

_____

_____

_____

THIS BROUGHT ME THE GREATEST JOY TODAY:

_____

_____

SOMETHING I DID TODAY THAT FELT MEANINGFUL:

_____

_____

_____

WHAT I DID TODAY THAT ALIGNED WITH MY PURPOSE:

_____

_____

_____

A NOTABLE RESULT FROM LIVING MY PURPOSE:

_____

_____

_____

A SETBACK I FACED TODAY AND HOW
I CAN LEARN OR GROW FROM THIS:

_____

_____

_____

_____

MORNING REFLECTION

DATE ___ / ___ / ___

MY PURPOSE OR INTENTION FOR TODAY:

_____

_____

_____

GOALS ALIGNED WITH MY PURPOSE:

_____   _____

_____   _____

_____   _____

ACTION STEPS I CAN TAKE TODAY:

☐ _____   ☐ _____

☐ _____   ☐ _____

☐ _____   ☐ _____

A SELF-CARE GOAL FOR TODAY:

_____

_____

A CHALLENGE I'M FACING: SOMETHING I'M EXCITED ABOUT:

_____   _____

_____   _____

_____   _____

HOW I SPENT MY TIME TODAY:

☐ MY LIFE'S PASSION   ☐ WORKING   ☐ TIME WITH FRIENDS/FAMILY

☐ VOLUNTEERING   ☐ SELF-CARE   ☐ TIME OUTDOORS

☐ ONLINE/SOCIAL MEDIA   ☐ DOWN TIME   ☐ OTHER: _____

EVENING REFLECTION

HOW I'M FEELING:

_____

_____

_____

THIS BROUGHT ME THE GREATEST JOY TODAY:

_____

_____

SOMETHING I DID TODAY THAT FELT MEANINGFUL:

_____

_____

_____

WHAT I DID TODAY THAT ALIGNED WITH MY PURPOSE:

_____

_____

_____

A NOTABLE RESULT FROM LIVING MY PURPOSE:

_____

_____

_____

A SETBACK I FACED TODAY AND HOW
I CAN LEARN OR GROW FROM THIS:

_____

_____

_____

MORNING REFLECTION

DATE ___/___/___

MY PURPOSE OR INTENTION FOR TODAY:

_____

_____

_____

GOALS ALIGNED WITH MY PURPOSE:

_____   _____

_____   _____

_____   _____

ACTION STEPS I CAN TAKE TODAY:

☐ _____   ☐ _____

☐ _____   ☐ _____

☐ _____   ☐ _____

A SELF-CARE GOAL FOR TODAY:

_____

_____

A CHALLENGE I'M FACING: SOMETHING I'M EXCITED ABOUT:

_____   _____

_____   _____

_____   _____

HOW I SPENT MY TIME TODAY:

☐ MY LIFE'S PASSION   ☐ WORKING   ☐ TIME WITH FRIENDS/FAMILY

☐ VOLUNTEERING   ☐ SELF-CARE   ☐ TIME OUTDOORS

☐ ONLINE/SOCIAL MEDIA   ☐ DOWN TIME   ☐ OTHER: _____

EVENING REFLECTION

HOW I'M FEELING:

_____

_____

_____

THIS BROUGHT ME THE GREATEST JOY TODAY:

_____

_____

SOMETHING I DID TODAY THAT FELT MEANINGFUL:

_____

_____

_____

WHAT I DID TODAY THAT ALIGNED WITH MY PURPOSE:

_____

_____

_____

A NOTABLE RESULT FROM LIVING MY PURPOSE:

_____

_____

_____

A SETBACK I FACED TODAY AND HOW
I CAN LEARN OR GROW FROM THIS:

_____

_____

_____

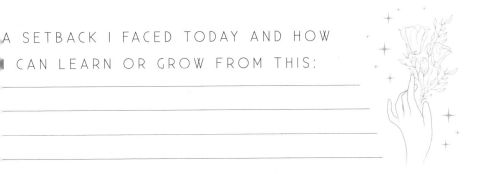

MORNING REFLECTION

DATE ___ / ___ / ___

MY PURPOSE OR INTENTION FOR TODAY:

_____

_____

_____

GOALS ALIGNED WITH MY PURPOSE:

_____   _____

_____   _____

_____   _____

ACTION STEPS I CAN TAKE TODAY:

☐ _____   ☐ _____

☐ _____   ☐ _____

☐ _____   ☐ _____

A SELF-CARE GOAL FOR TODAY:

_____

_____

A CHALLENGE I'M FACING: SOMETHING I'M EXCITED ABOUT:

_____   _____

_____   _____

_____   _____

HOW I SPENT MY TIME TODAY:

☐ MY LIFE'S PASSION   ☐ WORKING   ☐ TIME WITH FRIENDS/FAMILY

☐ VOLUNTEERING   ☐ SELF-CARE   ☐ TIME OUTDOORS

☐ ONLINE/SOCIAL MEDIA   ☐ DOWN TIME   ☐ OTHER: _____

EVENING REFLECTION

HOW I'M FEELING:

_____

_____

_____

THIS BROUGHT ME THE GREATEST JOY TODAY:

_____

_____

SOMETHING I DID TODAY THAT FELT MEANINGFUL:

_____

_____

_____

WHAT I DID TODAY THAT ALIGNED WITH MY PURPOSE:

_____

_____

_____

A NOTABLE RESULT FROM LIVING MY PURPOSE:

_____

_____

_____

A SETBACK I FACED TODAY AND HOW
I CAN LEARN OR GROW FROM THIS:

_____

_____

_____

_____

MORNING REFLECTION

DATE ___/___/___

MY PURPOSE OR INTENTION FOR TODAY:

_____

_____

_____

GOALS ALIGNED WITH MY PURPOSE:

_____   _____

_____   _____

_____   _____

ACTION STEPS I CAN TAKE TODAY:

☐ _____   ☐ _____

☐ _____   ☐ _____

☐ _____   ☐ _____

A SELF-CARE GOAL FOR TODAY:

_____

_____

A CHALLENGE I'M FACING: SOMETHING I'M EXCITED ABOUT:

_____   _____

_____   _____

_____   _____

HOW I SPENT MY TIME TODAY:

☐ MY LIFE'S PASSION   ☐ WORKING   ☐ TIME WITH FRIENDS/FAMILY

☐ VOLUNTEERING   ☐ SELF-CARE   ☐ TIME OUTDOORS

☐ ONLINE/SOCIAL MEDIA   ☐ DOWN TIME   ☐ OTHER: _____

EVENING REFLECTION

HOW I'M FEELING:

_____

_____

_____

THIS BROUGHT ME THE GREATEST JOY TODAY:

_____

_____

SOMETHING I DID TODAY THAT FELT MEANINGFUL:

_____

_____

_____

WHAT I DID TODAY THAT ALIGNED WITH MY PURPOSE:

_____

_____

_____

A NOTABLE RESULT FROM LIVING MY PURPOSE:

_____

_____

_____

A SETBACK I FACED TODAY AND HOW
I CAN LEARN OR GROW FROM THIS:

_____

_____

_____

_____

INSIGHTS

A Mandala Journal

MANDALA
PUBLISHING

www.mandalaearth.com

Art Direction and Design by Ashley Quackenbush